Challenges to Research Universities

Challenges to Research Universities

ROGER G. NOLL

Editor

Brookings Institution Press
Washington, D.C.

Copyright © 1998 by
THE BROOKINGS INSTITUTION
1775 Massachusetts Ave. N.W.
Washington, D.C. 20036

Library of Congress Cataloging-in-Publication data

Challenges to research universities / edited by Roger G. Noll.
p. cm.
Includes bibliographical references and index.
ISBN 0-8157-1510-2 (cloth : perm. paper).—
ISBN 0-8157-1509-9 (pbk. : perm. paper)
1. Universities and colleges—United States.
2. Research—United States.   3. Federal aid to higher
education—United States.   4. Federal aid to research—
United States.   I. Noll, Roger G.
LA227.4.C516   1997   97-21084
378.73—dc21   CIP

9 8 7 6 5 4 3 2 1

The paper used in this publication meets the minimum
requirements of the American Standard for Informational
Science—Permanence of Paper for Printed Library Materials,
ANSI Z39.48-1984

Typeset in Palatino

Composition by AlphaWebTech
Mechanicsville, Maryland

Printed by R.R. Donnelly and Sons Co.
Harrisonburg, Virginia

THE BROOKINGS INSTITUTION

The Brookings Institution is an independent organization devoted to nonpartisan research, education, and publication in economics, government, foreign policy, and the social sciences generally. Its principal purposes are to aid in the development of sound public policies and to promote public understanding of issues of national importance.

The Institution was founded on December 8, 1927, to merge the activities of the Institute for Government Research, founded in 1916, the Institute of Economics, founded in 1922, and the Robert Brookings Graduate School of Economics and Government, founded in 1924.

The Board of Trustees is responsible for the general administration of the Institution, while the immediate direction of the policies, program, and staff is vested in the President, assisted by an advisory committee of the officers and staff. The by-laws of the Institution state: "It is the function of the Trustees to make possible the conduct of scientific research, and publication, under the most favorable conditions, and to safeguard the independence of the research staff in pursuit of their studies and in the publication of the result of such studies. It is not a part of their function to determine, control, or influence the conduct of particular investigations or the conclusions reached."

The President bears final responsibility for the decision to publish a manuscript as a Brookings book. In reaching his judgment on competence, accuracy, and objectivity of each study, the President is advised by the director of the appropriate research program and weighs the views of a panel of expert outside readers who report to him in confidence on the quality of the work. Publication of a work signifies that it is deemed a competent treatment worthy of public consideration but does not imply endorsement of conclusions or recommendations.

The Institution maintains its position of neutrality on issues of public policy in order to safeguard the intellectual freedom of the staff. Hence interpretations or conclusions in Brookings publications should be understood to be solely those of the authors and should not be attributed to the Institution, to its trustees, officers, or other staff members, or to the organizations that support its research.

Foreword

The American system of higher education is unusual in many ways. In most of the world nearly all higher education is provided by large public institutions, but in the United States colleges and universities are remarkably diverse in their mission, ownership, scale, and scope. Among American colleges and universities, an elite set of about 100 institutions does many things in addition to educating students. These institutions perform most of the nation's basic research, provide a substantial amount of medical care (especially the most technically demanding services), and supply athletic entertainment to national television audiences. In most of the world, institutions of higher education serve primarily an educational purpose, leaving basic research, medical care, and athletics to other organizations.

Though American higher education has experienced periods of financial difficulty, the twentieth century has witnessed remarkable growth, especially since World War II. State governments have poured more and more dollars into public institutions to accommodate the steadily increasing number of young adults who desire higher education. The federal government has likewise supported higher education through grant and loan programs for students from lower-income families, educational benefits programs for veterans, basic research grants (especially in science and engineering), generous policies for reimbursing teaching hospitals for services provided to medicare patients, and income tax deductions for contributions to universities by businesses and individuals.

In the 1990s virtually all forms of public support for higher education began to decline. State appropriations for higher education began to shrink, and cost containment programs in health care turned many university medical centers into sources of major financial losses. Basic research grants to universities continued to grow in most fields, but in some major areas—especially engineering—federal support fell with the cutbacks in defense expenditures. Moreover, forecasts for reaching compliance with the agreement to balance the federal budget included significant cutbacks in university research after the year 2000. These trends have led some observers to wonder whether the golden era of the American research university is drawing to a close.

To assess the future of the research university, the Brookings Institution, through its Brown Center on Education Research, brought together a group of scholars to study the factors that are most likely to influence research universities in the coming years. The project was designed to assess the state of research universities with respect to their primary customers or client-supporters, including students, state and federal government, private industry, and third-party payers for medical services.

The problem facing research universities is not that they are performing poorly in terms of their primary social goals. The economic benefits of higher education are large and growing more rapidly than the increase in the cost of higher education, while an increasing proportion of the population attends college despite rising tuition and fees. In basic research and advanced medical services, U.S. institutions lead the world in new discoveries and useful inventions. Instead, the problem has been that state and federal governments have, until recently, seemed less willing to pay for most of these outputs of research universities. Universities have therefore turned to students (through tuition increases) and industry (through applied research collaborations) for an increasing fraction of their income.

These trends probably do not threaten the existence or dominance of elite American research universities, but they are likely to change their character substantially, even if Congress approves administration requests for enhanced federal support of university-based research. Among the conclusions reached by the authors of this study are that universities are likely to place more emphasis on education as they become more reliant on income from students and to withdraw from providing health services. In addition, the growing collaboration with industry may not be sustainable, for the desire for secrecy by industrial partners is incompatible with the broader educational and research missions of the university and may even destroy the value of university research to industry.

Early drafts of the chapters in this book were presented at a conference in June 1996 involving numerous experts on universities from academe and government. The conference and the publication of the book were sponsored by the Brown Center on Education Policy. Additional support for this project was provided by the Carnegie Corporation of New York. The authors are grateful for exceptional administrative support from Gemma Park, the inspiration and ideas of Lois Rice, and the generous assistance from colleagues in the Department of Education, the National Institutes of Health, and the National Science Foundation for guiding them through the confusing mountain of federal data on higher education. In addition they thank Steph Selice and Deborah Styles for editing the manuscript, Cynthia Iglesias and Helen Kim for verifying its factual content, Carlotta Ribar for proofreading, and Julia Petrakis for preparing the index.

The views expressed here are those of the authors and should not be ascribed to the trustees, officers, or staff of the Brookings Institution.

Michael H. Armacost
President

February 1998
Washington, D.C.

Contents

Chapter 1

The American Research University: An Introduction

Roger G. Noll

Amerian research universities have enjoyed a wonder-ful century, rising from a distinctly inferior status to world domination. But in the waning years of this golden age of American science and engineering, the future of these institutions is in doubt. This book explores in depth some of the major issues challenging the strength of U.S. research universities.

The concern that has been expressed by leaders of American higher education is hardly new. In 1983, the Academy of Political Science published a book entitled *The Crisis in Higher Education*, and the conclusion to its chapter on research universities began: "In order to continue in the style to which they have become accustomed, the research universities in both public and private sectors need a miracle."[1] In 1975 the *New York Times* proclaimed, "private colleges and universities . . . are, individually and collectively, in extreme danger," and the president of Dartmouth College opined: "I think the institution of private colleges and universities will survive, but . . . if present terms continue about half of them are going to go out of business."[2] A few years earlier, a detailed economic study of U.S. higher education was titled *The New Depression in Higher Education*.[3] One review of these assessments flatly stated the problem: "An accurate assessment of either the current or prospective financial situation of colleges and uni-

1

versities has thus far eluded those who have investigated the subject."[4] The skepticism of these authors was valid, for in the years that followed, American research universities enjoyed nothing short of a boom in both revenues and enrollments. Scholars who claim that the long-awaited crisis has finally arrived should approach this topic with humility.

The purpose of this book is to assess the condition and prognosis of American research universities. Our focus is on research universities because, since World War II, they have achieved unprecedented excellence in both education and research; yet in the past few years, several events have called their financial prospects into question. Among the more obvious problems are public controversies about financial management in universities and the integrity of academic research, cutbacks in federal research budgets, reduced state appropriations for higher education, the financial pinch on medical schools arising from managed care and other cost-containment policies in medical services, concerns that research and education are not sufficiently attuned to the needs of industry, and resistance among parents and political leaders to annual hikes in college tuition substantially in excess of the rate of inflation.

The remaining chapters of this book examine these issues in detail. In this chapter I set the stage by reviewing the current state of knowledge about the American research university.

Historical Background

Until the latter part of the nineteenth century, there were few American universities.[5] Only the oldest Ivy League institutions, established in the colonial era, and Thomas Jefferson's University of Virginia were respected; but even these were regarded as inferior to the great European universities. This only began to change after the Civil War.

Until the middle of the nineteenth century, the great universities were in Europe. The first institution that we would now probably recognize as a research university was Berlin University (1809), although a case can be made for the École Polytechnique

(1794).[6] In any case, German research universities were highly successful in producing skilled graduates who helped German industry become internationally dominant, especially in chemistry.[7]

The first important change in the United States was the creation of land grant state colleges through the passage of the Morril Act in 1862. This legislation was followed by the Hatch Act in 1887, which established the Agricultural Extension Service and federal support for crop research based at state universities.[8] Through these programs, numerous public institutions initiated research and technology transfer programs for agriculture, forestry, and mining. The mission of these universities included providing mass higher education with a strong focus on technical disciplines that were important to these industries.

The second major change occurred at the end of the nineteenth century, when the first generation of wealthy American industrialists financed the creation of great private research universities. After the passage of the income tax, the federal government enhanced the incentive to donate to universities by classifying them as charitable institutions and making donations to them tax deductible.[9] Between 1870 and 1920 the total number of faculty in American institutions of higher education increased ninefold, from 5,553 to 48,615, and the proportion of the population between 18 and 21 enrolled in institutions of higher education grew from 1.68 to 8.09 percent.[10] By the 1920s, the United States system of research universities was largely in place, and American institutions began producing more graduates than the universities of Europe. By World War II American universities were also regarded as equal to or better than the best universities in Europe.[11]

The role of the federal government in supporting higher education expanded dramatically during and immediately after World War II.[12] Even though the United States had created many high-quality research universities by the late 1930s, the contribution of the federal government to this effort was minuscule. Indeed, in 1940, the entire federal budget for research and development (R&D) was less than $75 million, of which $29 million (39 percent) was for agriculture, $26 million (35 percent) for defense,

$8 million (11 percent) for the Department of Interior, and $11 million for all other agencies.[13] By comparison, total research at universities was $27 million in 1940, not including administrative and facilities expenditures.[14]

During the war, arcane academic research in physical sciences and engineering found widespread practical use in military hardware. Consequently, the federal government perceived a national security advantage in generously supporting American research universities through a broad, decentralized system of project grants in science and engineering. Between 1940 and 1950, the contribution of the federal government to the income of universities increased from $39 million to $524 million.[15]

The postwar generosity of government toward universities went beyond supporting technical research in fields related to primary product industries and defense. From 1945 until the 1980s, the federal government adopted a series of programs to support research and education in virtually all fields, including the arts and humanities. Meanwhile, state governments dramatically expanded the system of public research universities.

Reflecting a belief that college education was both a key to personal success and of sufficient social value to merit public assistance, the federal government also initiated numerous programs to provide financial aid to students, starting with assistance to World War II veterans through the GI Bill. National Science Foundation fellowships for graduate study in technical disciplines were introduced, as well as guaranteed and subsidized student loans, and Pell grants and work-study assistance for undergraduates.[16] As discussed in chapter 2, state governments added to the largesse by vastly expanding the system of public higher education, creating new universities and converting others from largely teaching institutions to research universities. State subsidies of public universities account for more than 40 percent of their revenues—more than payments by students and their families, and far more financially significant than federal student aid.[17] Finally, both federal and state governments provide substantial other financial support to universities by paying for the relatively high cost of health care provided by medical schools, as examined in chapter 6.

As documented elsewhere in this book, the government-supported boom in American higher education apparently is coming to an end. The cause of this decline certainly is far deeper than any issue specifically related to the performance of universities. Allocations for all components of government-supported research are falling, in most cases more sharply than support for universities.[18] The most plausible cause of this downturn is the end of cold war justifications for sponsoring research that might have defense spillovers.[19] In addition, justifications based on long-term economic growth have failed to gain widespread political support.[20]

This book does not focus on these larger societal trends. Instead, it examines several key issues pertaining to the relationship between research universities and the rest of American society. Subsequent chapters analyze issues relating to the most important sources of income for universities: the overall trends in revenues and in state appropriations (chapter 2), tuition from students (chapter 3), federal research grants (chapters 4 and 5), medical services (chapter 6), and collaboration with industry (chapter 7). Conclusions are offered in chapter 8. This chapter provides some perspective on the rest of the book by discussing the defining characteristics of a research university and the rationale for maintaining a strong system of such institutions.

An Unusual Institution

A research university is a rare institution, both historically and internationally. This discussion is based on the assumption that these are its defining characteristics:

—Faculty are expected both to teach and to do research at a relatively high level of proficiency.

—The university backs up its research expectations by investing significantly in research facilities (such as libraries, laboratories, and computers).

—Teaching is diverse, including both the master-journeyman relationship in training new researchers and the general education of undergraduates, many of whom do not intend to make professional use of the material being taught by the teacher-researcher.

Of course, the boundaries between a research university and a teaching university (or between a university and a college) are indistinct, so that any definition of either boundary is arbitrary. A rough rule of thumb is that in a research university, faculty allocate somewhere between 25 and 75 percent of their effort to teaching, devote a significant part of teaching to students who seek advanced research degrees, are promoted and rewarded in great measure on the basis of their accomplishments in research, and generate outside support for this research that accounts for a substantial portion of the university's budget. The notion behind this definition is that the allocation of effort reveals not only the primary missions of the institution, but also the criteria likely to be used to make decisions in hiring and promoting faculty. If teaching effort is below this range, educational demands are not likely to play much of a role in staffing, and the organization is more appropriately regarded as a research institution that engages in some on-the-job training. Greater teaching effort is associated with institutions in which teaching is the only primary mission and the basis of staffing decisions, with research as a sideline.[21]

One attempt to distinguish research universities from other institutions of higher education was undertaken by a commission organized by the Carnegie Foundation.[22] This group used two criteria for defining a research university: the presence of doctoral programs, and significant amounts of federal grants. A third reasonable criterion is that a university offers doctorates and obtains research grants in several different disciplines. The last criterion excludes universities in which a medical school or an agricultural extension operation accounts for virtually all of its sponsored research.

Table 1-1 lists the research universities identified by the Carnegie Commission and the amount of research support each received from the federal government in fiscal 1994. The table shows both total federal support and the amount awarded through grants and contracts. The former number includes special grants for facilities, which vary substantially from year to year and are more susceptible to political influence regarding their geographic distribution than are peer-reviewed grants.

Table 1-1. *Research Universities and Federal R&D Funds,*
Fiscal 1994

Millions of dollars

University	Federal support		University	Federal support	
	Total	R&D grants		Total	R&D grants
Public—Carnegie					
Arizona State	31.1	25.3	U. Colorado	190.4	166.5
Auburn	32.5	19.2	U. Connecticut	52.2	44.8
Clemson	28.5	17.7	U. Delaware	32.4	26.1
Colorado State	67.0	56.6	U. Florida	93.7	73.0
Florida State	38.8	37.8	U. Georgia	66.9	48.9
Georgia Tech	89.8	51.4	U. Hawaii (Manoa)	58.7	50.6
Indiana	90.8	82.9	U. Houston	20.2	18.5
Iowa State	71.8	45.8	U. Idaho	21.7	15.8
Kansas State	31.7	20.6	U. Illinois (Chicago)	64.2	60.1
Kent State	8.0	7.0	U. Illinois (Urbana-Champaign)	146.6	119.7
Louisiana State	80.5	67.7	U. Iowa	100.5	94.5
Michigan State	86.0	67.4	U. Kansas	37.8	34.9
Mississippi State	36.9	20.5	U. Kentucky	65.4	48.6
New Mexico State	48.3	37.3	U. Maryland (College Park)	97.5	80.6
North Carolina State	72.9	50.0	U. Mass. (Amherst)	41.7	33.6
Ohio State	113.5	92.3	U. Michigan	263.2	240.4
Ohio U.	5.1	4.8	U. Minnesota	205.0	179.8
Oklahoma State	37.7	14.1	U. Mississippi	17.0	15.0
Oregon State	67.9	53.9	U. Nebraska	34.7	21.9
Penn State	207.4	184.4	U. New Mexico	74.4	58.3
Purdue	97.4	77.9	U. North Carolina	165.1	146.6
Rutgers	80.8	64.4	U. Oklahoma	32.5	28.2
So. Illinois (Carbondale)	10.1	8.0	U. Oregon	25.0	20.0
SUNY Albany	15.6	15.3	U. Pittsburgh	159.2	152.9
SUNY Buffalo	45.5	37.9	U. Rhode Island	26.4	18.8
SUNY Stony Brook	66.5	61.8	U. South Carolina	28.6	22.0
Temple	32.5	28.3	U. South Florida	28.3	25.7
Texas A&M	89.3	59.7	U. Tennessee	40.8	24.6
Texas Tech	7.0	6.5	U. Texas (Austin)	124.1	103.1
U. Alabama (Birmingham)	112.3	104.4	U. Utah	98.8	84.9
U. Arizona	157.9	144.0	U. Vermont	40.0	34.9
U. Arkansas	23.8	17.7	U. Virginia	84.5	76.4

Table 1–1. *continued*

| University | Federal support | | University | Federal support | |
	Total	R&D grants		Total	R&D grants
U. Calif. Berkeley	180.8	148.8	U. Washington	310.0	275.9
U. Calif. Davis	104.1	98.9	U. Wisconsin (Madison)	238.4	207.6
U. Calif. Irvine	69.5	66.1	U. Wisconsin (Milwaukee)	6.9	5.6
UCLA	236.5	221.8	U. Wyoming	18.4	12.8
U. Calif. Riverside	21.1	19.4	Utah State	45.7	38.4
U. Calif. San Diego	233.1	218.3	Virginia Commonwealth	45.6	41.6
U. Calif. San Francisco	217.5	204.4	Virginia Tech	51.3	38.4
U. Calif. Santa Barbara	64.9	60.0	Washington State	43.8	30.6
U. Calif. Santa Cruz	19.6	18.2	Wayne State	49.3	45.4
U. Cincinnati	55.4	52.4	West Virginia	31.1	22.2

			Public—Not Carnegie		
CUNY City College	15.0	13.9	U. Alaska (Fairbanks)	36.1	31.7
Florida A&M	17.6	12.7	U. Central Florida	12.3	10.7
Montana State	25.2	16.8	U. Maine	16.0	10.4
North Carolina A&T	18.4	10.8	U. Missouri	47.1	29.3
San Diego State	15.1	11.4	U. Nevada (Reno)	15.7	12.5
San Jose State	14.8	10.2	U. New Hampshire	22.2	19.2
U. Alabama (Hunts.)	23.6	21.9	U. North Dakota	17.1	10.7

			Private—Carnegie		
Boston U.	84.5	77.8	Northwestern	106.1	99.9
Brandeis	21.1	19.3	Princeton	67.3	62.0
Brigham Young	6.1	5.5	Rensselaer	27.3	20.6
Brown	39.7	37.0	Rice	30.0	26.5
Caltech	109.1	83.8	Rockefeller	43.7	42.4
Carnegie Mellon	70.0	66.5	St. Louis	22.3	20.6
Case Western Reserve	108.2	99.5	Stanford	282.5	262.4

Table 1–1. *continued*

Millions of dollars

| University | Federal support | | University | Federal support | |
	Total	R&D grants		Total	R&D grants
Columbia	197.6	187.3	Syracuse	18.5	16.7
Cornell	221.5	194.5	Tufts	47.4	45.1
Duke	165.5	154.6	Tulane	41.3	40.9
Emory	78.3	75.4	U. Chicago	114.7	102.4
George			U. Miami	88.9	83.7
Washington	25.4	23.3			
Georgetown	62.5	61.1	U. Notre Dame	17.1	16.0
Harvard	210.0	190.1	U. Pennsylvania	209.1	190.3
Howard	25.1	19.8	U. Rochester	125.9	108.6
Johns Hopkins	764.0	612.7	U. Southern Calif.	166.2	149.9
Lehigh	14.0	12.9	Vanderbilt	98.1	87.2
MIT	290.3	267.4	Washington U.	165.3	149.9
New York U.	98.1	92.8	Yale	200.8	182.8
Northeastern	12.6	12.1	Yeshiva	76.1	71.3
		Private—Not Carnegie			
Clark Atlanta	25.8	22.1	Stevens Inst. Tech.	11.5	11.2
Dartmouth	41.5	40.1	U. Dayton	33.6	29.4
Drexel	10.3	10.0	Wake Forest	56.8	51.8
Illinois Inst.					
Tech.	16.0	10.8			

Source: U.S. National Science Foundation, *Federal Science and Eneginering Support to Universities, Colleges, and Nonprofit Institutions: Fiscal Year 1994*, NSF Publication 96-317, Arlington, Virginia: National Science Foundation, pp. 56-78. The list of Carnegie research universities was obtained from the web site: http://cause-www.colorado.edu/member-dir/institutions_by_carnegie.html

Table 1-1 also lists twenty-one other universities (fourteen public and seven private) that perform at least as much federally sponsored research as the bottom group of the Carnegie research universities. The criterion for including these universities was solely whether they received more than $10 million in federal research grants. All of these schools undertake more federally sponsored research than at least six of the Carnegie research universities.[23] In addition, the Carnegie list includes five universities in which nearly all sponsored research is accounted for by a medical school: Emory, St. Louis, the University of California at San Francisco, Virginia Commonwealth, and Yeshiva. All twenty-one of the universities not classified as research universities obtain more research support for activities outside of a medical school than do these six.

These data clearly reveal that the precise number of research universities depends on definitions, and the weights accorded to the three criteria determine which universities among a marginal group of about thirty would be included. Whereas a few of the Carnegie universities probably should be excluded, at least an equal number plausibly could be added. We can then conclude that the United States has around 125 such institutions.

Of course, the intensity of research and the prestige of these institutions varies widely. In 1993, the federal government awarded $10.94 billion in science and engineering research grants to universities and colleges. Ten large universities received nearly 23 percent of this amount ($2.48 billion), and thirty-three universities received half of the total.[24] The concentration of grants in the top institutions has declined in recent years, but only slightly. For example, in 1986, the federal government spent $6.46 billion in grants to universities, of which about 24 percent went to the top ten institutions and half to the top thirty-one universities.

An International Perspective

The United States does not have a monopoly on research universities, but it is remarkably dominant and has been for several decades. Other large, wealthy nations have at most a few universities that are serious research institutions. For the most part the systems in other nations differ from the U.S. system in five fundamental ways.

Numbers

On a per capita basis, other nations have fewer universities. Although Europe was the home of the first great universities, the number of such institutions in these countries is remarkably small: seventy in Germany, seventy-six in the United Kingdom (including thirty polytechnic schools that were recently given university status), and forty-one in Spain.[25]

In general, other nations have not made as great an investment in their university systems. For example, in Germany real expenditures and faculty size for universities have been stagnant since the 1970s.[26] In France, only the *grandes écoles* have fared reasonably well in the budgetary process, and they account for only a small fraction of the students in natural science and engineering; for the system as a whole, budgets have not kept pace with enrollments.[27] In Britain, only the universities at the top of the system are equipped to provide world-class education, and universities as a whole are starved for resources in comparison with those in the United States and the rest of Europe.[28]

A frequent complaint about university education in other countries is that it does not adequately prepare students for jobs as technologists in private industry because it is too theoretical. In response, several governments created polytechnic institutions or new practical training programs within universities that combine characteristics of vocational education with those of college.[29] Some countries upgraded technical-vocational schools to university-like status. These programs were intended to increase the supply of technically skilled employees. Polytechnics produce a significant proportion of degrees in science and engineering, including about half those awarded in Germany and half in the United Kingdom.[30] Likewise, in Italy most of the expansion in higher education has been in three-year programs designed to produce technically skilled employees for industry.[31]

Enrollment

Reflecting the differences in the number of universities, the proportion of young adults attending an institution of higher education is far higher in the United States than in the rest of the world. One method for ascertaining the relative importance of higher education in universities is to measure the proportion of young adults achieving an objective standard of formal learning. The Organization for Economic Cooperation and Development (OECD) has developed one such measure and estimates the proportion of students who achieve each of five levels: Level 5 (usually outside a university, and of shorter duration and lower quality than a college degree); Level 6 (first full university degree); and Level 7 (postgraduate education). Otto Keck has used OECD data to calculate the proportion of students who terminate their education after achieving each of these levels, and his data are reproduced in table 1-2. As is apparent, formal university education plays a substantially bigger role in the United States than in other large countries. Table 1-3 shows the proportion of 24-year-olds who have received a first degree. Except for Canada and Norway, no other nation approaches the United States in the proportion of young adults who have graduated from college. In 1992, the 20- to 24-year-old age cohort numbered 35.0 million in Europe and 18.8 million in the United States, whereas total university enrollment was 11.4 million in Europe and 14.5 million in the United States.

In recent years, other nations have expanded their systems of higher education more rapidly than the United States. Total enrollment in higher education in the United States increased from 11.3 million in 1975 to 14.5 million in 1991; however, in the European Economic Communities (EEC), the increase was from 5.5 million to 9.9 million in the same period, more than double the U.S. rate.[32] The growth in enrollment in Europe applies to almost all countries, including France, Germany, and the United Kingdom, with the only exceptions being some of the former Warsaw Pact nations. In Asia, enrollments in higher education increased dramatically between 1975 and 1990. Enrollment quintupled in China and South Korea and nearly doubled in India and Taiwan; however, in Japan enrollment grew more slowly than in the United States, increasing from 2.25 million to 2.65 million.[33]

Degrees

The concentration of higher education degrees in the natural sciences and engineering is far higher in the rest of the world than in the United States, especially since Europeans have begun to place emphasis on using mass higher education to produce a more technically sophisticated work force. In 1992, 9.7 percent of

Table 1-2. *Educational Achievement Levels in Postsecondary Education, 1986–87*

	Percentage of age group qualifying at		
Country	Level 5	Level 6	Level 7
Australia	9.7	16.5	1.6
Canada	13.3	24.5	4.1
France	14.7	15.3	6.2
Germany	7.7	12.4	1.5
Italy	0.4	7.9	1.4
Japan	11.1	21.9	1.5
Norway	36.3	16.1	7.3
Spain	0.1	14.7	0.5
United Kingdom	12.3	14.2	4.6
United States	12.7	24.1	9.7

Source: Otto Keck, "The National System for Technical Innovation in Germany," in Richard R. Nelson, editor, *National Innovation Systems: A Comparative Analysis*, New York: Oxford University Press, 1993, p.140, derived from Organization for Economic Cooperation and Development, *Education in OECD Countries, 1986-87*, Paris: Organization for Economic Cooperation and Development, 1989.

U.S. college graduates had a degree in natural sciences and 5.4 percent in engineering, compared with 14.7 and 13.8 percent, respectively, in the European Union.[34] In 1990 in Japan, 6 percent of first degrees were in science and 20 percent in engineering; in South Korea, the comparable figures are 14 and 17 percent, respectively.[35] Because so many U.S. students are in college, the proportion of 24-year-olds with a first degree in engineering or natural sciences is higher in the United States than in the EEC. However, this lead is not large, and several nations equal or surpass the United States in the proportion of students in these fields, including Canada, Japan, Korea, and the United Kingdom.

The total number of U.S. students in science is comparable to that in Europe (table 1-4). In 1992, U.S. institutions awarded 111,000 first degrees in science compared with 123,000 in Europe. The major difference is in engineering, where European institutions awarded 117,000 degrees, compared with 62,000 in the United States; even so, the ratio of engineering degrees to the size of the age cohort is roughly comparable. Moreover, as was ex-

Table 1-3. *Proportion of 24-Year-Olds with University Degree, 1992*[a]

Region/Country[b]	Number of 24-year-olds	Percentage of age group qualifying at natural science/engineering	
		First degree	First degree
Asia[c]	43,717,235	3.8	1.2
China	25,017,278	1.2	0.6
India	15,545,800	4.8	1.1
Japan	1,868,387	23.4	6.2
South Korea	871,581	20.5	6.7
Taiwan	361,789	15.0	5.9
Europe[d]	7,432,867	13.5	4.0
EEC	5,877,146	14.0	4.0
Denmark	78,432	16.0	4.7
Finland	74,371	16.7	6.4
France	858,554	13.0	4.2
Germany	1,376,072	12.8	5.0
Italy	921,010	10.4	2.3
Spain	660,040	19.5	3.5
United Kingdom	898,580	20.8	5.6
Non-EEC	1,555,721	11.7	4.0
Bulgaria	117,381	20.3	7.6
Czech Rep.	146,187	12.4	5.7
Norway	67,800	30.9	3.8
Poland	515,925	10.7	2.8
Romania	381,306	7.8	5.2
Slovak Rep.	78,627	13.6	7.4
North America	5,896,393	24.0	4.1
Canada	388,426	29.6	5.3
Mexico	1,753,814	8.4	2.8
U.S.	3,754,153	30.6	4.6

Source: U.S. National Science Foundation, *Human Resources for Science and Technology: The European Region*, NSF Pub. 96-316, Arlington, Virginia: National Science Foundation, 1996, p. 77.
[a]Or most recent year before 1992.
[b]Among countries for which data are available, includes countries with more than 300,000 twenty-four-year-olds, plus other countries with high proportions of university graduates.
[c]Asia total also includes Singapore.
[d]Does not include the former Soviet Union, the Balkan nations, and Turkey.

plained previously, the European totals include some (but not all) graduates of polytechnic programs, which produce degrees not really comparable to engineering degrees from universities in either Europe or the United States.

Table 1-4. *Number of University Degrees, 1992*
Thousands

Region/ Country	First university degree			Doctorates		
	All	Natural science	Engineering	All	Nastural science	Engineering
Asia	1,725.3	242.9	280.8	25.6	6.6	4.6
China	298.4	34.0	120.8	1.8	.5	.8
India	750.0	147.0	29.0	8.4	3.7	.6
Japan	437.9	26.5	88.4	11.6	1.8	2.4
South Korea	178.6	26.7	31.8	3.2	.5	.6
Taiwan	54.4	7.5	9.5	.6	.2	.3
Europe	1,004.5	140.1	158.9	47.1	19.0	6.4
EEC						
France	111.8	17.9	17.8	8.2	4.6	1.2
Germany	176.7	29.9	38.9	21.4	6.7	2.1
Italy	96.2	13.1	7.9	2.7	.8	.3
Sweden	15.9	1.6	2.4	1.7	.5	.4
U.K.	178.7	29.6	18.8	8.4	3.9	1.3
Non-EEC						
Hungary	13.1	1.1	1.3	.6	.3	.1
Norway	20.9	.5	2.1	.4	.2	.1
Poland	55.4	6.9	7.4	1.5	.6	.4
Switzerland	9.2	1.5	.8	2.1	.7	.1
North America						
Canada	114.9	13.4	7.1	2.9	.8	.4
U.S.	1,150.1	111.2	61.9	39.8	12.6	5.7

Source: U.S. National Science Foundation, *Human Resources for Science & Technology: The European Region*, NSF Pub. 96-316, Arlington, Virginia: National Science Foundation, 1996, pp. 77, 84.

A similar pattern exists for doctorates. In 1992, the United States awarded about two-thirds as many doctorates in natural sciences as did European universities, and almost as many doctorates in engineering. In Europe, the number of doctorates in engineering and natural sciences is roughly 8 percent of the number of first degrees, whereas in the United States it is more than 10 percent. Because some first European degrees are somewhat more advanced than a first U.S. degree, these figures probably imply no difference between Europe and the United States in the distribution of degrees in terms of the duration and intensity of study.

As with enrollments, the number of degrees in natural sciences and engineering is growing much more slowly in the

United States. Between 1975 and 1991, the number of first degrees awarded in natural sciences actually fell in the United States (from 117,000 to 111,000), while it more than doubled in the EEC (53,000 to 121,000). In engineering, first degrees in the United States increased from 40,000 to 62,000, while in the EEC the number of such degrees more than doubled, from 50,000 to 114,000.[36] In Asia, the number of bachelor of science degrees in natural science grew from 128,000 in 1975 to 253,000 in 1990, while the number of engineering graduates grew from 93,000 to 261,000.[37]

Decentralization

Government support for fundamental research is more fragmented and decentralized in the United States, with much greater emphasis on the market-like features of competitive, peer-reviewed research proposals from individual researchers. In some nations, research in a particular field is likely to be centrally managed, and (even among universities) to be parceled out among institutions in a top-down fashion, derived from formulas based on output measures.[38] In other cases, the centerpiece of the basic research system is national laboratories, which are inherently more centralized in budgeting and project prioritization. University faculty engage in research through affiliations with these institutions. An example is the Max Planck Society, which is composed of several scientific research institutes that participate in postgraduate education in universities.[39] A similar system has been developed in France.[40]

Private support for universities, whether individual donations or research grants from companies and foundations, is almost unknown everywhere except the United States. In the rest of the world, almost all universities are public, and essentially all university budgets are accounted for by government appropriations. These processes tend to be formal, rigid, and hierarchical, rather than competitive and peer-reviewed. For example, in France, universities have virtually no discretion in research activities, and, as state enterprises, are subject to the formal administrative and employment rules of the French system of public administration.[41] In the United Kingdom, departmental budgets are set by the central ministry, based on formulas related to enrollments and publications.[42] The system in Germany is similarly rigid. A government report in 1988 concluded that the entire German system of research was at risk because of the decline of its research universities brought on by lack of financing and poor administration.[43]

National Laboratories

The system of national laboratories differs between the United States and other advanced, industrialized democracies in scope, scale, and management. For example, in the United States approximately 10 percent of national R&D effort is conducted in federal agencies and installations, and another 5 percent in national laboratories managed by private companies, universities, or nonprofit research institutions.[44] About two-thirds of the budget for privately managed national laboratories goes to labs that are run by universities.

By contrast, in France, the National Committee for Scientific Research (CNRS) operates 1,000 laboratories that account for 22 percent of total national R&D effort. These labs employ half of all scientists and engineers in France who are engaged in basic research. In addition, France participates in several joint research laboratories within the European Union, including several high-energy physics facilities.[45] Only a handful of French universities are seriously engaged in a broad spectrum of research in natural sciences and engineering, and even in these cases the work tends to be done in separate research institutions that are divorced from teaching.[46]

In Germany, reunification gave the government the impetus to make substantial investments in new research institutions in the east, and the emphasis was placed on national laboratories. The German government opened three new national research centers in the east (focusing on molecular medicine, geology, and the environment) and branch institutes of thirteen more national research centers.

Because of the emphasis on national laboratories in other nations, research and education are more separated. As a result, in rankings of the leading research institutions within a particular field of science and engineering, most of the world leaders in the United States are universities, whereas most of the world leaders elsewhere are government research laboratories.[47] The reason for this phenomenon is that in the United States about 70 percent of the authors of scientific and technical publications are affiliated with academic institutions.[48] In Europe, university faculty frequently have associations with research laboratories, but these labs are physically separated from universities and the research typically is identified with a laboratory, not a university. This physical separation serves to make faculty less accessible to students and to attenuate the link between universities and the research reputations of its faculty.

The management of many U.S. government-owned research institutions by universities and other independent entities is rare elsewhere. The arrangements between the U.S. federal government and universities to manage major national laboratories that undertake applied R&D, including the development of nuclear weapons and advanced spacecraft, is unique in the world. In 1994, the federal government spent more than $5 billion in nineteen federal laboratories that were managed by universities.[49] The important distinction here, of course, is that unlike the circumstances with national laboratories in Europe, U.S. universities manage the laboratories, and in so doing also manage the relationships between the labs and both faculty and students.

Implications

This summary of the state of universities throughout the world is quite sobering. American universities clearly are well off compared to nearly all of their international competitors. Whereas enrollments are mushrooming in the rest of the world, resources for higher education have not kept pace. Scholars from these countries uniformly express deep concern about the resulting quality of education. Basic research in other countries has grown. But because this research is generally conducted in national laboratories, it has not had a spillover benefit for higher education, even though many of the researchers in national labs are also university professors.

One important consequence of the unique nature of the American research university is that in the United States education and research in science and technology are more integrated, especially in experimental areas of science and engineering that require laboratories. Conventional wisdom regards research and education as distinct, conflicting activities; in Europe, recent history seems to reflect the belief that the two can be managed quite separately and inconsistently. The European system of education is expanding rapidly, but not the budget for education; the system of national laboratories receives the bulk of the funds for research, and its relatively plush financial state is largely disconnected from education.

The uniqueness of U.S. research universities derives from their integration of teaching and research. Were education and research completely separate, employment as a faculty member in a research university would resemble having two part-time jobs, one as a teacher and the other as a researcher. (This circumstance is not far from the case in much of Europe.) Indeed, the view that research and education are largely substitutes for one another, competing for faculty time, is reflected in the popular criticism that faculty devote too much time to research and not enough to students.

In practice, a plausible case can be made that research and education have strong complementarities. In laboratory sciences, students are crucial to the success of research programs. Many students work in university research laboratories, either as paid research assistants or in unpaid positions earning academic credit. For example, in 1991, 74,000 graduate students in natural science and engineering were employed as research assistants, whereas 101,000 holders of doctorates in these fields were employed by academic institutions and had R&D responsibilities.[50]

For faculty who work in disciplines where research involves neither teamwork nor support from assistants, the view that teaching and research are substitutes may be accurate in that education and research do exhibit more conflict than complementarity. Even in these disciplines, however, faculty who are active researchers have some advantages as teachers, an issue discussed in detail in chapter 3. In the academic disciplines that receive almost all government financial support, a substantial part of the work in university research laboratories is done by students, and a great deal of teaching is in the context of mentoring relationships within a research project. As a result, the key issue in evaluating research universities is the importance of the complementarity between research and education.

Rationales for Supporting Research Universities

Many rationales have been given for why the United States ought to maintain a system of research universities. The most plausible rationale is the one that to many seems least believable: excellence in research enhances the quality of education in science and engineering.

Before proceeding, an important caveat must be stated. Relatively little research has been undertaken that addresses the social payoff of university research. A great deal has been written to explain why research is important and to demonstrate that American universities produce a great deal of highly respected work. But this work cannot support some sort of global assessment of the productivity of research universities, much less address the question of whether there are too many or too few of them.

The most commonly cited rationales for supporting research universities focus on the case for undertaking R&D.[51] The two main reasons are that the output of R&D projects—new technical knowledge—is a form of public good, and that the federal government needs to support R&D in areas where it is a monopsony consumer or monopoly supplier.

The public goods argument refers to the ability of the person or organization undertaking research to retain proprietary control over the new information that is discovered, especially in areas of fundamental research defining the technology base of an industry. To the extent that private R&D is motivated by the prospect of financial reward, a purely private system of R&D will underinvest in areas where new knowledge is hard to keep proprietary. The federal procurement and production rationale refers to areas in which government dominates the market, the most obvious example of which is national security. The argument here is that to minimize costs and obtain optimal quality, the government must support research.

In both cases, the rationale for government-sponsored work includes the advantages of disseminating new information widely, rather than trying to keep it proprietary. Whereas the producer of new technology derives maximum benefit from proprietary knowledge, the mechanism by which this is made possible is the creation of technological monopolies. Like all monopolies, those based on new technology have the disadvantage that they create inefficiencies. Monopolies generally cause prices to exceed the incremental cost of production; as a result, they exclude some end users from enjoying the benefits of the innovation. In addition, secure property rights in new technology can prevent others from making further innovations that use the technology. Finally, a monopoly with secure proprietary knowledge in the technology of an industry (and a relatively impregnable barrier to market entry against competitors) can have less of an incentive to engage in further innovation (the so-called "Arrow Effect").[52] Allowing widespread access to R&D outputs maximizes their dissemination, including the rate of technological progress in the economy and the extent to which end users (rather than innovators) derive the benefits of technological progress.

Some important work demonstrates that university research has had a high social payoff. Chapter 7 reviews recent studies of this type. Of course, this research suffers from a serious handicap. Because the vast majority of university research in science and engineering is fundamental, tracing out exactly how it affects innovation elsewhere in society is difficult and bound to understate the effect.

An even more serious difficulty is that demonstrating that university research produces net economic benefits proves at best that fundamental research of a kind done at universities is worthwhile—not that most of it should be done there, rather than in government labs, private industry, or nonprofit research institutions. In the end, the case for supporting research universities must depend on the productivity of university research efforts and the unique feature of these institutions: that they integrate teaching and research in a way that makes at least one of these activities more productive.

An important part of the rationale for supporting higher education is that it increases the earning potential of students. Chapter 3 examines this issue in some detail. Because these payoffs accrue to the students, one might expect them to bear the burden of financing their education. However, for three reasons, society might decide to subsidize higher education:

—Students may not be able to afford investments in education that yield high returns, in part because they come from low-income families or because their lack of collateral limits access to loans.

—Because taxes are positively related to income, subsidies for higher education may be financed all or in part by greater tax collections from the higher incomes of college graduates.

—If society underinvests in R&D because the results are not fully captured by the innovator, and if education plays an important role in enabling students to do R&D, the wages of educated students will not fully reflect their social productivity. Subsidizing their education, then, can serve to encourage more people to prepare themselves for research careers that the labor market will tend to undervalue.

Though these rationales, if valid, can justify subsidies for higher education, they do not warrant special subsidies for attending research universities. Research universities are advantaged by federal programs that subsidize higher education. Federal aid to students, such as through Pell grants and the GI Bill, is based partly on tuition charges. The standard approach is to base aid on financial need, which is defined as the difference between the cost of higher education and the student's and family's ability to pay.[53] As a result, students generally qualify for more financial aid at institutions that charge higher tuition. In addition, federal research grants typically pay part of the tuition costs of students who work on federally supported projects. These grants go almost exclusively to research universities. Finally, the federal government makes numerous training grant awards. These grants are awarded on the basis of peer review and, like research grants, are highly concentrated among research universities.[54]

Giving research universities an advantage in subsidies for higher education makes sense only if these universities add more value for their students. It is worth noting that in Europe, a significant fraction of science and engineering education is in polytechnic institutions that are not research universities and that, in many cases, do not produce graduates who are qualified for advanced study. The rationale for the current pattern of student support in the United States, like the rationale for supporting university research, therefore depends on whether education and research are complements rather than substitutes for one another. Thus, to justify an extensive investment in research universities requires demonstrating that research and education exhibit economies of scope—that is, that the productivity of one activity is enhanced by the presence of the other.

Unfortunately, relatively little research has focused on the issue of complementarities between research and education. Chapter 3 summarizes the remarkably small amount of research on the comparative earnings of graduates of different types of institutions of higher education. This work does support the proposition that research universities are more productive suppliers of higher education. Likewise, the success of U.S. universities in attracting foreign students in technical disciplines (also discussed in chapter 3) suggests that the unique combination of research and education found at so many American universities produces more attractive educational opportunities.

In addition, the substantial amount of corporate support for university research inferentially supports the conclusion that research universities are unique providers of some types of research. Corporations presumably support university R&D because it is profitable to do so, despite two fundamental problems. A corporation must sacrifice some managerial control if it chooses to support work in another institution rather than perform it in house. In addition, inevitably, corporations will be less able to keep research results proprietary if the research is performed outside the company. In fact, for these reasons corporations perform virtually all research in house and rarely pay for research performed elsewhere.[55]

So strong is the desire not to share proprietary information that many firms in high-tech industries either refuse to participate in government programs or separate their government contract work from research in support of commercial activities. For example, five of the ten leading semiconductor manufacturers will not sell to the government; in the computer industry, many firms have separate government divisions.[56] Likewise, recent attempts to encourage corporate sponsorship of research in national laboratories have not been successful.[57] However, political as well as technical and economic factors are responsible for this result.[58] Nevertheless, as discussed in chapter 2, corporations do spend substantial amounts at universities. In recent years, industry has provided between 5 and 10 percent of university research funds (nearly $1.5 billion).

Though all of this information is consistent with the view that federal support for research universities is justified, the case is certainly not proved. More research must be done on the nature of the higher education production function—and, in particular, the extent to which it exhibits complementarities between research and education—before a strong conclusion can be supported.

The Book's Agenda

The remainder of this book examines several significant issues pertaining to the future of the American research university. The general organization of the book focuses on the most important sources of income for universities: federal grants, state appropriations, student payments through tuition and postgraduation gifts, third-party payors for medical services that are provided by universities, and corporate research sponsors.

Chapter 2 provides a general conceptual overview of the operation of research universities, discussing their objectives and primary constituencies (or customers). This chapter also examines state appropriations for higher education, which is the primary source of support for public universities.

The relationship between universities and students is addressed in chapter 3, focusing on how to measure the success of research universities in serving students. (This book does not contain an analysis of student financial aid, a topic addressed extensively in other Brookings books. As a result, we focus here on other issues.)[59]

Chapters 4 and 5 deal with federal research grants. Chapter 4 examines the long-term budget outlook for federal expenditures on grants to universities, and chapter 5 discusses indirect cost recovery, an important source of conflict between universities and the federal government.

Perhaps the least appreciated aspect of university operations is the focus of chapter 6: the provision of health care services in connection with medical schools. Medical services are an important source of revenues, and for the past two decades profits from medical services have paid for a great deal of university research. This chapter explores the effect medical schools have on the operation and financial prospects of research universities.

Chapter 7 summarizes recent research on the relationship between universities and private industry and presents new evidence on how university research benefits corporations.

This book explores many themes, and the individual chapters offer numerous conclusions about trends in university operations and proposals for policy change. These conclusions are summarized in chapter 8. One theme permeates several chapters: the future of the research university is cloudy. All sources of revenues for the research university seem to have reached a plateau or even to have begun to decline. The biggest declines are in two important sources of support for research: state appropriations and profits from medical services. Federal grant support also has begun to shrink.

If these trends persist for a long time, universities can be expected to de-emphasize research in science and engineering: to shrink faculties in these areas, and not to replace research facilities as they become obsolete. The more prestigious universities probably will remain research institutions, but they will reduce the proportion of their activities that involve the kinds of relatively expensive research that accounts for the bulk of federal grants to universities. These universities will come to resemble institutions that now rank lower in both intensity of research and prestige. The less prestigious research universities are likely to stop trying to be serious research institutions in experimental science and engineering.

Unfortunately, the present state of knowledge about the productivity of research universities does not permit many robust conclusions about the implications of this trend. Certainly the dominant role of U.S. universities in research prestige and in educating foreign scholars can be expected to slip. The extent to which this occurs will be determined by decisions in other countries concerning their support for universities and other research institutions. In addition, the fragmentary evidence indicates that the productivity and earnings of graduates of research universities can be expected to drop.

At this time the analysis of research universities is too fragmentary to say whether the United States currently over- or underinvests in research universities. Consequently, one cannot offer a firm conclusion about whether these trends represent a serious long-term threat to American economic growth or simply a correction to an overly enthusiastic program of support in the recent past. Of course, all research projects seem bound to conclude that still more study is needed, and this one is no exception. Nevertheless, one conclusion is clear: barring a dramatic and unexpected reversal in current trends, the American research university faces its most serious, long-term financial challenge since World War II, and probably its most momentous in history.

Endnotes

1. Joseph Froomkin, "The Research University," *The Crisis in Higher Education: Proceedings of the American Academy of Political Science*, vol. 35, no. 2 (1983), p. 46.

2. Quoted, with some irony, in David W. Breneman and Chester E. Finn Jr., "An Uncertain Future," in David W. Breneman, Chester E. Finn

Jr., and Susan C. Nelson, eds., *Public Policy and Private Higher Education* (Brookings, 1978), p. 3.

3. Earl F. Cheit, *The New Depression in Higher Education: A Study of Financial Conditions at 41 Colleges and Universities* (McGraw-Hill, 1971).

4. Breneman and Finn, "An Uncertain Future," p. 9.

5. For more details on the history of American universities, see Jacques Barzun, *The American University: How It Runs, Where It's Going* (Harper & Row, 1968); David D. Henry, *Challenges Past, Challenges Present: An Analysis of American Higher Education since 1930* (San Francisco: Jossey-Bass, 1975); and Nathan M. Pusey, *American Higher Education 1945–70: A Personal Report* (Harvard University Press, 1978).

6. Otto Keck, "The National System for Technical Innovation in Germany," in Richard R. Nelson, ed., *National Innovation Systems* (Oxford University Press, 1993). The École Polytechnique was a center of scientific research in the Napoleonic era, but its academic program then, as now, did not emphasize experimental science and engineering. See François Chesnais, "The French National System of Innovation," in Nelson, *National Innovation Systems*, p. 197.

7. David C. Mowery and Nathan Rosenberg, "The U.S. National Innovation System," in Nelson, *National Innovation Systems*, p. 35.

8. Mowery and Rosenberg, "The U.S. National Innovation System," p. 37. For a more thorough history of the agricultural research program, see R. E. Evenson, "Agriculture," in Richard R. Nelson, ed., *Government and Technical Progress: A Cross-Industry Analysis* (Pergamon, 1982), pp. 233–82.

9. For a summary of the tax status of gifts to universities and colleges, see Emil M. Sunley Jr., "Federal and State Tax Policies," in Breneman, Finn, and Nelson, *Public Policy and Higher Education*, p. 285ff.

10. U. S. Department of Commerce, Bureau of the Census, *Historical Statistics of the United States: Colonial Times to 1957* (1960), p. 211.

11. Mowery and Rosenberg, "The U.S. National Innovation System," pp. 35–36.

12. See Nelson, *Government and Technical Progress*, which examines the history of federal support for commercially relevant research in universities and elsewhere; and Linda R. Cohen and Roger G. Noll, *The Technology Pork Barrel* (Brookings, 1991), chapters 1 and 2, which summarizes the history of large-scale, mission-oriented commercial R&D by the federal government.

13. Mowery and Rosenberg, "The U.S. National Innovation System," p. 35.

14. Department of Commerce, *Historical Statistics*, p. 213.

15. Ibid., p. 212.

16. For annual data on expenditures for student aid programs and a detailed history of their evolution, see Lawrence E. Gladieux and Arthur M Hauptman, *The College Aid Quandary: Access, Quality, and the Federal Role* (Brookings, 1995), pp. 8–11, 14–23.

17. Gladieux and Hauptman, *The College Aid Quandary,* p. 3.

18. These trends are documented in the annual compendium from the National Science Foundation, *Federal R&D Funding by Budget Function* (Arlington, Va., 1996).

19. In 1990, universities accounted for 57 percent of the basic research for the Department of Defense, and ninety-two universities ranked among the top 500 defense contractors. See Ann Markusen and Joel Yudken, *Dismantling the Cold War Economy* (Basic Books, 1992), p. 110.

20. Linda R. Cohen and Roger G. Noll, "Research and Development after the Cold War," in Judith B. Sedaitis, *Commercializing High Technology: East and West* (Lanham, Md.: Rowman and Littlefield, 1997).

21. The best liberal arts colleges require some research proficiency in promotions, differing from research universities primarily in that they generally do not engage in graduate education. In many fields, the best liberal arts colleges have prominent research scholars. However, these institutions do not spend significant amounts in laboratory science and engineering and do not receive substantial federal research grants.

22. *A Classification of Institutions of Higher Education: A Technical Report Sponsored by the Carnegie Commission on Higher Education* (New York: Carnegie Foundation for the Advancement of Teaching, 1973). The Carnegie Commission defined two categories of universities: Research I—the top fifty universities in federal grants and contracts in two of the three years between 1968–69 and 1970–71 that granted at least fifty doctoral degrees in 1969–70; and Research II—universities in the top 100 federal grant recipients that granted more than fifty doctorates, or other universities ranking among the top fifty in doctoral degrees. See Breneman, Finn, and Nelson, *Public Policy and Private Higher Education,* p. 452.

23. Brigham Young, Kent State, Ohio University, Southern Illinois at Carbondale, Texas Tech, and the University of Wisconsin at Milwaukee receive less in federal grants than these other universities.

24. These data refer to the research universities that are shown in table 1-1. The thirty-four universities that receive the most in federal grants include one single-purpose medical school, Baylor College of Medicine, which is excluded from table 1-1 and is not included in the top thirty-three schools cited in the text. Data cited in this paragraph are from National Science Foundation, *Federal Science and Engineering Support to Universities, Colleges, and Nonprofit Institutions: Fiscal Year 1993,* NSF Doc. 95-331 (Arlington, Va., 1994), table B-4.

25. National Science Foundation, *Human Resources for Science and Technology: The European Region*, NSF Doc. 96-316 (Arlington, Va., 1996), pp. 25, 38, 44.

26. Keck, "The National System for Technical Innovation in Germany," p. 141.

27. Chesnais, "The French National System of Innovation," pp. 210–211.

28. William Walker, "National Innovation Systems: Britain," in Nelson, *National Innovation Systems*, pp. 178–80.

29. National Science Foundation, *The European Region*, pp. 25–58, contains country profiles of higher education systems in Europe that makes reference to the developments summarized in this paragraph, especially in France, Germany, and the United Kingdom. In many countries, the expansion of technical education has not been accompanied by an expansion of the number of permanent, full-time faculty.

30. Ibid., pp. 26, 38.

31. Ibid., p. 42.

32. Ibid., pp. 85–86.

33. National Science Foundation, *Human Resources for Science and Technology: The Asian Region*, NSF Doc. 93-303 (Washington, 1993), pp. 61–62.

34. National Science Foundation, *The European Region*, pp. 80–81.

35. National Science Foundation, *The Asian Region*, p. 90.

36. National Science Foundation, *The European Region*, p. 87.

37. National Science Foundation, *The Asian Region*, p. 63.

38. Martin Trow, *Trust, Markets and Accountability in Higher Education: A Comparative Perspective* (Berkeley, Calif.: University of California, Graduate School of Public Policy, 1996), p. 3.

39. Keck, "The National System for Technical Innovation in Germany," p. 141.

40. Chesnais, "The French National System of Innovation," p. 210.

41. Ibid., p. 210.

42. Trow, *Trust, Markets and Accountability in Higher Education*.

43. Keck, "The National System for Technical Innovation in Germany," p. 141.

44. National Science Board, *Science & Engineering Indicators—1993*, NSB 93-1 (Government Printing Office, 1993), p. 331.

45. National Science Foundation, *The European Region*, pp. 35–36.

46. Chesnais, "The French National System of Innovation," p. 210.

47. For a summary of data about the dominance of U.S. research universities and comparisons with research institutions elsewhere, see Linda R. Cohen and Roger G. Noll, "Research and Development," in Henry Aaron and Charles L. Schultze, eds., *Setting Domestic Priorities: What Can Government Do?* (Brookings, 1992), pp. 223–66.

48. National Science Board, *Science & Engineering Indicators—1993*, p. 428.

49. National Science Foundation, *Academic Science and Engineering R&D Expenditures*, NSF Pub. 95-332 (Arlington, Va., 1995), p. 187.

50. National Science Board, *Science & Engineering Indicators—1993*, pp. 406, 415–17.

51. For a more complete review of the case for government support for research, see Cohen and Noll, *The Technology Pork Barrel*, chapter 2.

52. Kenneth J. Arrow, "Economic Welfare and the Allocation of Resources for Invention," in National Bureau of Economic Research, *The Rate and Direction of Inventive Activity: Economic and Social Factors* (Princeton, N.J.: Princeton University Press, 1962), pp. 609–26.

53. Michael S. McPherson and Morton Owen Schapiro, *Keeping College Affordable: Government and Educational Opportunity* (Brookings, 1991), pp. 4ff.

54. In 1993, the federal government awarded $525 million in fellowships, traineeships, and training grants, of which $113 million (22 percent) went to the universities ranking in the top ten in research grants. This fraction is only slightly lower than the share of research grants (23 percent) acquired by these universities. See National Science Foundation, *Federal Support to Universities*, table B-9.

55. Kirk Monteverde and David Teece, "Supplier Switching Costs and Vertical Integration in the U.S. Automobile Industry," *Bell Journal of Economics*, vol. 13 (1982), pp. 206–213.

56. John A. Alic and others, *Beyond Spinoff: Military and Commercial Technologies in a Changing World* (Boston: Harvard Business School Press, 1992), pp. 149–53, 181–182, 335.

57. Government labs are regarded by companies as among the least significant sources of corporate innovations. See Lawrence M. Rausch, "R&D Continues to Be an Important Part of the Innovation Process," *National Science Foundation Data Brief*, no. 7 (August 7, 1996).

58. Linda R. Cohen and Roger G. Noll, "Feasibility of Effective Public-Private R&D Collaboration: The Case of Cooperative R&D Agreements," *International Journal of the Economics of Business*, vol. 2 (1995), pp. 223–40.

59. Gladieux and Hauptman, *The College Aid Quandary*. See also McPherson and Schapiro, *Keeping College Affordable*.

Chapter 2

Universities, Constituencies, and the Role of the States

Linda R. Cohen and Roger G. Noll

The American research university is a complex organization, pursuing several objectives and serving various
constituencies. Like all nonprofit organizations, universities must espouse public service goals if they are to retain their
tax-exempt status. Nevertheless, universities and other nonprofit
institutions bear many similarities to more prosaic for-profit businesses because their survival depends on acquiring sufficient revenues to offset their expenses. To maintain a healthy relationship
between revenues and expenditures, universities must be successful in marketing their products and controlling their costs.

The purpose of this chapter is to explain the goals and operations of research universities and how these are affected by the
ways in which universities generate income. We first discuss
university goals and management and how universities can be
expected to respond to significant changes in the level and composition of demand for their services. We then briefly examine
recent trends in the pattern of financial support for universities
and discuss in more detail the factors that influence state appropriations for research universities. The chapter thus serves two
main purposes: to establish a general conceptual model of university operations that is useful for understanding the implications
of the other chapters in the book, and to examine an important

31

source of support for universities—appropriations by state governments.

Objectives and Organization of Research Universities

As nonprofit, tax-exempt institutions, universities are required to have a formal statement of purpose that justifies their special status. Although each research university puts the matter a little differently, these statements of purpose typically incorporate three separate items: education, research, and community service. The statements take the form of lofty but vague general pronouncements. Nevertheless, they are significant in that a university must justify all of its activities as serving these broad public purposes to retain its tax-exempt status. Of course, the tax status of universities is extremely important. Tax exemption frees universities from the obligation to pay almost all taxes (although typically universities do volunteer to make payments in lieu of taxes to local governments in the community where they are located) as long as the income they derive from their activities is used for these public purposes. Tax exemption also enables private donors to universities to claim their gifts as tax-deductible contributions. For a wealthy person who lives in a state with a high personal income tax, the tax deductibility of university gifts can reduce the effective cost of a contribution by 40 percent or more. Universities therefore have a powerful incentive to make certain that their activities are congruent with their public service objectives.

Both university personnel and the general public discuss universities and their relationships with students, alumni, government, and private donors in terms of these goals; however, uncritical acceptance of them as the sum and substance of a university is misleading and sometimes counterproductive. It is unrealistic to expect that the objectives of universities are perfectly congruent with the public purposes that motivate both the tax exemptions and the federal programs that support universities. For two fundamental reasons, the goals of universities and government are certain to diverge. Universities have numerous constituencies other than the government, and inevitably they must make trade-offs among the various demands of these constituencies. In addition, the nature of a university prevents it from being governed by a representative cross-section of society, which causes its values and purposes to differ from those of voters and their political representatives. Each of these points deserves some elaboration, for they provide considerable insight into why the relationship between universities and government is bound to involve conflict.

Financial Incentives

Although government provides much of the financial support for research universities, it is not the only important source of support. To survive and prosper, universities must satisfy numerous constituencies. In this sense, a university, and for that matter any nonprofit institution, has many similarities with a for-profit firm. Universities must succeed at marketing their products to those who pay for them and must keep their costs within the bounds of their revenues.

The main differences between nonprofit and for-profit organizations is how they spend their "surplus"—the amount by which revenues exceed the minimum costs of providing services to their customers. For-profit firms call this surplus profit and either pay it out to stockholders in dividends or reinvest it to expand their profit-making activities. Payments to stockholders and additional earnings from reinvested profits must be sufficient to induce private investors to hold equity in the company, or else the firm eventually will go out of business. In practice, if markets for final products and managerial control of corporations are not perfect, managers may retain some of this surplus for themselves in salaries and perquisites.

For nonprofit institutions, the surplus is, theoretically, spent on additional nonremunerative public services. However, as with for-profit firms, managers may retain some of the surplus for themselves if competition among nonprofit organizations (and for nonprofit managers) is not robust. Before discussing the issue of the treatment of the surplus, we first elaborate on the ways in which universities are like for-profit firms because of the discipline imposed on them by market realities and financial constraints.

If he who pays the piper calls the tune, the key to understanding the prioritization of activities by research universities is revealed in their sources of revenues.[1] The most salient feature of the income of research universities is its enormous diversity. Table 2-1 shows the distribution of revenues from 1975 through 1995 among the Research I and Research II universities that wcre identified by the Carnegie Commission on Higher Education, as discussed in chapter 1.[2]

The two most important sources of revenue are tuition and state and local government appropriations. Tuition includes payments by and on behalf of students by other entities, such as private foundations and governmental financial aid programs. For the purposes of identifying the separate customers and constituencies of universities, lumping these funds together makes sense, because students control the decision about which universities receive these payments through their decisions about where to enroll.

State and local government appropriations provide financial support for operations and capital investments. Nearly all of these funds are provided by state government and go to public universities.[3] To some extent, these appropriations are based on enrollment and are sensitive to the ability of state-supported universities to attract students. However, part of these appropriations are for supporting activities that are not sensitive to enrollments or that are not directly connected to education, such as state-supported research programs and university-based community services.

Another source of revenues related to students is gifts. In table 2-1, gifts are included with contracts. Gifts refer to income from nongovernmental sources that is not part of endowment, while the endowment column reflects the amount of income from endowment that is available to universities to spend in a given year. This latter figure is somewhat arbitrary, for universities are free to set their own payout rate from endowment, although this rate must exceed 4 percent if the university is to retain its tax-exempt status. As with state appropriations, these two categories lump together gifts with three quite different purposes (whether for operations or endowment): educational (such as to provide scholarships or student housing); general research (such as to finance a new facility to house a scientific laboratory); and project grants from wealthy individuals, businesses, and private foundations. In the last case, sometimes private donors are allowed to retain a property right or right of prior notification in the research they sponsor. For 1994–95, among all universities and colleges (not just research universities, as in table 2-1), 28 percent of gifts to universities came from alumni, 23 percent from other individuals, 20 percent from corporations, 19 percent from foundations, and 9 percent from other organizations.[4]

The last category of revenue that is associated with education is sales of educational activities. This revenue comes from educational activities not associated with normal degree programs, such as seminars, extension courses, and executive training programs. These revenues are not associated with standard undergraduate and graduate degree programs, and they reflect a source of competition with mainstream educational activities for the attention of university personnel.[5]

Table 2-1 reveals the other customers of research universities besides regular students in degree programs. Research is obviously a highly important activity. Federal grants and contracts are used almost entirely to support research in science, engineering, and medicine. Likewise, an unknown fraction of state appropriations, gifts, and endowment income also supports research. In 1995 probably at least 25 percent of the income of a research university was directly related to its research.[6] In addition, part of the income derived from students is also related to research in that some students, especially those seeking technical degrees, select universities on the basis of the quality of their research activities.

The least appreciated fact about the modern research university is the significance of activities that involve neither research nor teaching in regular degree programs.

Sales of medical services actually are more important to research universities than are research grants from the federal government and are comparable in importance to tuition. The president of a major research university that has a medical school is not

Table 2-1. Sources of Current Funds Revenues at Research Universities

Millions of current dollars

Year	Tuition and fees	State and local government appropriations	Federal grants and contracts	Private gifts and contracts	Endowment income	Sales of educational activities	Auxiliary enterprises	Hospital revenues	Independent operations	Total current funds revenues
1975	2,391	4,376	2,740	868	425	395	1,667	1,372	1,037	16,227
1976	2,653	4,870	2,930	952	402	468	1,852	1,561	1,004	17,707
1977	2,900	5,284	3,097	1,036	442	578	1,998	1,765	1,391	19,549
1978	3,171	5,845	3,288	1,160	488	643	2,185	2,011	798	20,800
1979	3,476	6,445	3,669	1,258	566	762	2,344	2,307	949	23,125
1980	3,864	7,128	4,220	1,412	655	897	2,659	2,745	1,087	26,230
1981	4,438	7,764	4,674	1,607	740	1,016	2,993	3,188	1,198	29,368
1982	5,094	8,447	4,698	1,807	833	1,136	3,385	3,730	1,188	32,183
1983	5,861	8,848	4,764	2,110	901	1,240	3,631	4,283	1,320	34,878
1984	6,436	9,581	5,126	2,308	985	1,410	3,947	4,693	1,492	38,113
1985	6,959	10,789	5,629	2,593	1,105	1,512	4,247	4,927	1,683	41,898
1986	7,656	11,690	6,233	2,914	1,223	1,681	4,571	5,419	1,920	46,025
1987	8,492	11,947	6,894	3,187	1,192	1,863	4,856	5,929	2,631	49,903
1988	9,285	12,738	7,336	3,510	1,309	2,050	5,166	6,910	2,474	53,878
1989	10,189	13,587	8,046	3,908	1,479	2,359	5,484	7,866	2,551	59,015
1990	11,162	14,390	8,687	4,409	1,585	2,566	5,957	8,718	2,681	63,949
1991	12,221	14,839	9,195	4,715	1,703	2,875	6,349	9,915	2,835	68,738
1992	13,450	14,684	10,011	5,103	1,803	3,237	6,657	11,187	3,004	73,357
1993	14,448	14,595	10,741	5,510	1,959	3,446	7,200	11,784	3,019	77,065
1994	15,433	14,953	11,538	5,818	1,982	3,568	7,706	12,291	2,955	80,709
1995	16,417	15,691	12,107	6,082	2,142	3,855	8,026	12,585	3,052	84,990

Millions of constant 1996 dollars

Year										
1975	6,660	12,190	7,633	2,418	1,184	1,100	4,645	3,822	2,889	45,204
1976	6,870	12,612	7,587	2,465	1,042	1,211	4,797	4,043	2,600	45,858
1977	6,942	12,647	7,413	2,481	1,057	1,334	4,782	4,225	3,330	46,791
1978	7,056	13,004	7,316	2,581	1,085	1,431	4,861	4,474	1,774	46,275
1979	7,123	13,209	7,520	2,577	1,160	1,561	4,804	4,728	1,944	47,394
1980	7,257	13,388	7,927	2,653	1,231	1,685	4,994	5,155	2,042	49,266
1981	7,564	13,232	7,966	2,739	1,261	1,731	5,102	5,433	2,041	50,053
1982	8,080	13,398	7,451	2,866	1,321	1,802	5,370	5,916	1,884	51,047
1983	8,933	13,486	7,261	3,216	1,374	1,890	5,533	6,528	2,012	53,159
1984	9,389	13,977	7,477	3,367	1,437	2,056	5,758	6,846	2,176	55,597
1985	9,786	15,172	7,915	3,646	1,553	2,126	5,971	6,927	2,366	58,915
1986	10,455	15,963	8,512	3,980	1,671	2,296	6,242	7,400	2,621	62,851
1987	11,261	15,842	9,141	4,226	1,581	2,470	6,439	7,862	3,488	66,171
1988	11,885	16,304	9,390	4,493	1,676	2,624	6,612	8,844	3,167	68,960
1989	12,486	16,651	9,860	4,789	1,812	2,891	6,720	9,639	3,127	72,324
1990	13,063	16,841	10,167	5,160	1,855	3,003	6,972	10,203	3,138	74,843
1991	13,779	16,731	10,368	5,316	1,921	3,242	7,159	11,179	3,196	77,505
1992	14,849	16,213	11,053	5,635	1,991	3,574	7,349	12,351	3,317	80,992
1993	15,576	15,734	11,579	5,940	2,112	3,715	7,762	12,704	3,254	83,080
1994	16,319	15,812	12,200	6,153	2,095	3,772	8,148	12,997	3,125	85,343
1995	16,901	16,154	12,464	6,261	2,205	3,969	8,263	12,957	3,142	87,497

Source: NSF/Caspar Institutional Data File at URL http://caspar.nsf.gov/ accessed 12/1/97. Research activities based on Carnegie RI and RII schools, as coded by Caspar, omitting nonstudent entries. Constant dollars calculated using a fiscal year GDP deflator, reported in National Science Board, Science and Engineering Indicators, 1996, appendix table 4-1, p. 102.
aDue to accounting changes, the categories are not strictly compared before and after 1987. See the NSF/Caspar website for details about these changes.

only the leader of an academic enterprise, but he or she frequently is also the CEO of a large medical service corporation that collects hundreds of millions of dollars for providing medical care. Not surprisingly, our experiences in academic administration at two very different research universities, Stanford and the University of California, have been that issues involving university medical centers consume a huge fraction of the attention of high-level administrators. These issues greatly influence university policies concerning budgets, financial control, and personnel management.

Likewise, sales of other services are important, producing roughly the same amount of income as do gifts and endowment. This category covers a variety of activities, including intercollegiate athletics, communications and computer services, campus retail outlets such as bookstores and restaurants, fees for managing national laboratories, royalties from licensing intellectual property owned by the university, and numerous other business activities.

To ascertain the relative financial incentive for education versus research requires separating state and local appropriations, private gifts and grants, and endowment income according to their purpose. For all colleges and universities, federal grants and contracts account for about 60 percent of all R&D. Other institutional funds account for 18 percent, and the remainder is divided in roughly equal amounts among appropriations from state and local governments, industry, and other private sources.[7] Thus, R&D effort in 1993 among research universities amounted to about $20 billion, or more than 25 percent of revenues. In addition, sales of services other than normal degree programs accounted for $22 billion, or about 30 percent of revenues. Tuition plus the portion of state and local appropriations that is not for research accounted for about $27 billion, or 35 percent of revenues. If anything, these figures overstate the importance of education to universities, because some students (especially those in technical disciplines) probably select universities partly on the basis of their reputations in research. To criticize research universities and their faculty for not devoting most of their attention to students ignores an important financial reality: most of the funds received by universities are not for the purpose of educating students.

Universities engage in activities other than education and research for many reasons. Some activities, such as intercollegiate athletics and on-campus retailing, are important to students and donors and part of the competition among universities for students and gifts. In other cases, universities engage in activities that are natural extensions of operations that are part of or necessary to their primary missions, such as selling communications and data analysis services. In still other cases, education and research naturally complement related services. University health care is an obvious case in point. Half of the four years of medical school is devoted to on-the-job training in hospitals and clinics, and a significant component of research involves clinical trials on patients.

Like the relationship between education and research, the connections between both and the provision of services raises issues of whether these activities complement the main mission of the university or deflect attention from it. Chapter 6 examines this issue in detail with respect to medical services, where the case for complementarities has recently been challenged. A similar debate arises with respect to the educational compromises made by many universities in pursuit of excellence in (and substantial profits from) intercollegiate athletics.

The more subtle inference from this excursion into university finances is that, regardless of the extent to which these activities complement or substitute for one another, research universities are deeply involved in many activities. Indeed, their financial health is at stake in a broad spectrum of activities other than simply educating students. Moreover, to the extent that these activities create a surplus—that is, the counterpart to profits in a for-profit organization—the resources available for education actually may be larger, not smaller, because of this diversification. In short, research universities have diversified in part because they have been paid a great deal to do so, and they probably could not withdraw from these activities without suffering considerable financial pain.

Table 2-1 also provides useful information about the trends in the revenues of American research universities. Whereas research universities have been diversified for a long time, the distribution of income among the various categories has changed substantially. Total revenues of research universities were roughly five times as great in 1995 as in 1975, having grown about 10 percent per year during this period. Slightly less than half of this growth is accounted for by general inflation in the economy. The rest represents real growth in the size and scope of activities.

The only revenue item that has grown at roughly the same rate as total revenues is endowment income. The items that have grown substantially more rapidly than total revenues are tuition, gifts, sales of educational activities, and medical care sales. The activities that have grown more slowly than total income are state appropriations, federal grants and contracts, and auxiliary activities. Moreover, state appropriations fell in inflation-adjusted dollars from 1987 to 1993. There has been some increase in the past two years, but in real terms state support in 1995 was still lower than in 1988. Federal grants and hospital sales grew in real terms throughout the period, but (as discussed in chapters 4 and 6) are now falling and are expected to do so for several more years.

These trends reveal some interesting features of the changes in the demands placed on research universities. Tuition has only recently become the most important source of revenues, surpassing state appropriations for the first time in 1993 and federal grants in 1982. The declining share of revenues accounted for by federal grants and contracts has not been offset by growth in gifts and endowment income. Whereas hospital sales grew enormously over this period, creating surpluses that primarily benefited medical education and medical research, this source of support is now disappearing. Finally, if federal grants decline substantially during the next few years, it is quite likely that gifts and endowment will surpass federal grants in financial significance. This implies a considerable reorientation of university research programs away from public (and largely open) research and toward private (and more frequently proprietary) projects, raising important questions about the role of universities that are discussed in chapter 7.

University Priorities

At this point, it is appropriate to return to the question of the true goals of a university and its decisions about how to spend its surplus of revenues over costs. The significance of this issue is that it provides the key to understanding how universities are likely to respond to declining revenues in some but not all of their activities. To illustrate the point, if the United States suddenly lost interest in intercollegiate football so that games of Division I powerhouses no longer earned millions of dollars from television, ticket sales, and concessions, almost certainly most universities would cut back their football programs rather than try to maintain them at the present level by cutting back on education and research expenditures. The issue that motivates this section is to separate the activities that, like football, are undertaken primarily to generate income and public support for the university from those activities that universities would work hard to maintain if revenues from them declined.

Most likely, universities have earned surpluses from federal support for research in science and engineering and the sale of health care and various other services outside mainstream undergraduate and graduate education. As explained in chapter 5, the surplus from science and engineering grants accrues through the so-called indirect costs of research incorporated into research grants. And, as explained in chapter 6, the explosion in university medical services helped finance a large fraction of the costs of research and education in medical schools, including a major portion of the salaries of clinical faculty. A plausible explanation for the trends in the revenues of research universities is that universities have invested to some degree in both technical research and various noneducational services as a means for financing education and other research. To develop the case for this interpretation of the evolution of the research university requires examining how universities are governed and what this implies about their priorities.

The formal governance structure of universities is somewhat misleading. Ultimate management responsibility lies with a governing board, either politically appointed regents (for a public university) or a self-perpetuating group of alumni and principal donors (for a private university). The board typically approves the budget, new academic and research programs, and all faculty and administrative appointments, including the president (or chancellor), the academic vice president (or provost), deans of schools, and even chairs of academic departments. Nevertheless, as a practical matter, the most powerful force in running universities is the body of tenured faculty.

Universities espouse academic freedom, which means that faculty control the content of classroom instruction, the character of individual research projects, and faculty publications. Likewise, senior faculty are responsible for the adoption and continuation of academic tenure. This system protects faculty from dismissal for reasons other than grossly inappropriate behavior and gives faculty members considerable authority in promotion and retention.

The importance of academic freedom and tenure in influencing university governance is immense. One consequence of the tenure system is that universities are extremely decentralized. The day-to-day operation of education and research is decentralized to programs and in many cases to individual faculty. These units obtain their financial resources in part from the central university budget and in part from their own fund-raising activities. A second consequence is that academic administrators have only limited ability to change the activities of programs. Whereas academic administrators do initiate programs and influence academic life, their initiatives must receive the support of tenured faculty to succeed. Academic freedom guarantees that faculty cannot be forced to participate in these programs, and tenure assures that changes in the composition of faculty (in particular, through recruitment—perhaps the area where administrators have the most authority) will be slow. And finally, regardless of the formal division of responsibilities, administrators are largely selected by the faculty, almost always from within their own ranks.

To understand the objectives of research universities, then, requires understanding the collective objectives of its faculty. These objectives are complex, but are certainly not fully captured by the lofty ideals espoused in the incorporation documents of research universities. Most faculty like to teach and to do research, but they are also motivated by personal ambition. Like everyone else, they seek economic rewards and prestige, and part of their efforts in education and research are motivated by these personal objectives. One can therefore expect universities to be motivated by the same goals: to enhance the economic rewards to their faculty and to seek prestige as an end in itself, beyond its value in attracting students, grants, and gifts.

As collective decisionmaking entities, a key to understanding the formation of institutional goals is to count the number of faculty in various academic units. Statistics on the disciplinary distribution of university faculty turn out to be surprisingly difficult to come by—perhaps because no federal legislation requires their collection. Tables 2-2 and 2-3 present some data for the 1972–73 and 1992–93 academic years. The 1992–93 data are derived from a survey of faculty performed by the National Center for Education Statistics. The "research university" category is based on the same set of universities that were identified by the Carnegie Commission and listed in table 1-1. For the 1972 data, the universities were not identified as the Carnegie set, so table 2-3 compares the earlier data to all Ph.D.-granting institutions in 1992–93. In addition, the 1972–73 data are classified by the field of highest degree of faculty, and the 1992–93 data are classified by principal field of teaching. Important distortions that result from this definitional difference are discussed further below. In general, only conclusions based on gross differences between the two years are appropriate.

Table 2-2 shows that, for all research universities, about 60 percent of the faculty, and nearly two-thirds of the tenured faculty, are in the fields that obtain virtually all external research support: the sciences (including agriculture and medicine) and engineering. This actually overstates the fraction of faculty who work in departments that obtain a large amount of grant support, as some of the disciplines within social sciences (virtually all of the social sciences except for psychology) and natural sciences (for example, mathematics) obtain few research grants.[8] Thus, in most universities, including the highly prestigious Ivy League schools, the best public institutions, and other prestige private universities such as Chicago and Stanford, the decision to invest substantial resources in the most lucrative fields of science, engineering, and medicine has been made by institutions in which a

Table 2-2. *Distribution of Faculty and Instructional Staff in Research Universities by Discipline, 1993*

Percent (unless otherwise specified)

Principal field of teaching	All research universities			Public research universities			Private research universities		
	All faculty	Tenure track	Tenured	All faculty	Tenure track	Tenured	All faculty	Tenure track	Tenured
Business	4.7	4.8	4.3	4.1	4.5	4.2	6.2	6.0	4.7
Education	5.4	4.7	5.0	7.0	5.6	5.9	1.4	1.1	1.3
Fine arts	6.0	5.3	5.5	5.6	5.0	5.1	7.0	6.4	7.4
Humanities	10.4	10.1	11.2	10.4	10.2	11.1	10.4	9.8	11.8
Social sciences	10.2	11.6	11.8	9.4	10.9	11.0	12.2	14.2	15.5
Engineering	6.6	8.8	8.3	7.8	9.4	8.8	3.7	6.6	6.1
Agriculture	4.7	6.8	7.4	6.3	8.2	8.8	0.8	1.7	1.5
Natural sciences	17.5	21.7	22.8	17.6	20.8	21.8	17.5	24.9	27.6
Health sciences	23.7	17.6	15.1	21.4	16.4	14.7	29.5	22.1	17.3
All other fields	10.7	8.7	8.6	10.4	9.0	9.0	11.3	7.2	6.8

Source: National Center for Education Statistics, 1993 *National Survey of Post-Secondary Faculty*, computation by DAS-T Version 0.50 (January 28, 1997, and February 5, 1997).

Table 2-3. *Faculty and Instructional Staff, 1972–73 and 1993*

	All institutions				Universities			
Discipline	1972–73		1993		1972–73		1993	
Business	24	5	81	8	8	4	18	5
Education	65	13	81	8	20	9	20	6
Fine arts	43	8	72	7	16	7	20	5
Humanities	87	17	150	15	31	14	37	10
Social sciences	69	13	101	10	31	14	37	10
Engineering	40	8	40	4	23	11	20	5
Natural sciences and agriculture	107	21	202	20	50	22	76	21
Biological sciences and agriculture	38	7	n.a.		22	10	n.a.	
Physical sciences	69	13	n.a.		27	12	n.a.	
Agriculture	n.a.		19	2	n.a.		12	3
Natural sciences w/o agriculture	n a		183	18	n.a.		64	18
Health sciences	17	3	150	15	15	7	96	26
Other	65	13	142	14	28	13	40	11
Total faculty	519		1,108		222		363	

Sources: Alan E. Bayer, "Teaching Faculty in Academe: 1972–73," *ACE Research Reports*, vol. 8, no. 2 (August 1973), pp. 26–27, National Center for Education Statistics, *1993 National Survey of Post-Secondary Faculty*.

Note: Data for 1972–73 are by field of highest degree, and 1993 data are by principal field of teaching.

n.a. = Not available.

majority of faculty work in other fields. The financial presumption at these universities is that departments of history and literature, and schools of education, law, and public policy, have flourished in part because of the excess revenues generated by technical disciplines.

Both tables 2-2 and 2-3 give some indications that the allocation of faculty has—slowly—responded to changes in funding opportunities. The most striking difference between the two surveys shown in table 2-3 is the growth in health sciences faculty. Even if some (or all!) of the faculty identified in 1972 as in the "biological sciences" (by field of degree) taught in health sciences, so that they would appear in the health sciences category in the 1992 survey, the relative size of the field's faculty grew significantly, paralleling the huge increase in sales at hospitals as a source of revenue for universities. Of course, the shares of faculty by field must sum to 100 percent, so other disciplines need to show a decline as a share of faculty. The reported disciplinary categories lack precision (it is particularly unfortunate that we could not distinguish between physical sciences and life sciences in 1993), but it seems reasonable to hypothesize that the relatively larger decline in the share of engineering faculty at universities followed the reduced importance of federal grants to university financing.

It is, of course, hardly surprising that faculty shares shift with grant support. If the changes that seem reflected in table 2-3 are correct, the information about tenured faculty in table 2-2 suggests that universities may have a hard time adjusting to the expected declines in federal research support and hospital profits. In particular, the fields responsible for most federal grant activity twenty years ago (engineering and natural sciences) are disproportionately tenured, particularly at private universities. The health sciences are the major exception; however, while health sciences account for "only" 17.3 percent of tenured faculty at private universities, compared with nearly 30 percent of all private university faculty, this share represents phenomenal growth from twenty years ago. In all of the fields where grant income has been important, universities have a huge, built-in financial commitment because of academic tenure. Although universities can terminate tenured faculty by eliminating departments and programs, because universities are largely run by tenured faculty, and because so many tenured faculty are in these fields, the problem of downsizing and reallocating resources in response to declining income will be difficult to solve.

Financial Management

The majority of funds for supporting educational activities, whether tuition payments by students or gifts to the university for educational purposes, accrue to the central administration—either the university as a whole or the school within the university in which a student is enrolled. The sources of funds for research are more balanced. Most funds for long-term capital investments for research usually accrue to the central administration, and most funds to support the operating costs of research are raised through grants to individual faculty. Typically, the central administration imposes a "tax" on these grants, called indirect costs or overhead, which are discussed in greater detail in chapter 5. Whereas these taxes are based on accounting estimates of the costs of administration and facilities that are devoted to research activities, as a practical matter the revenues so collected flow into the operating budget of the university and are allocated among academic and administrative units by the central administration.

Central budget decisions of research universities naturally tend to favor academic units that do not have access to other substantial means of support. Typically, units that receive substantial amounts of grants and gifts have larger total expenditures per faculty member in all areas, including clerical staff and graduate students. However, budget support for these departments from the university administration is usually smaller than for disciplines that do not receive grants. As a result, the overall budgetary impact on an academic unit from successfully raising its own funds is to have this revenue partly offset by reductions in its central operating budget. In short, as collective decisionmaking institutions, universities are egalitarian, redistributing income from "rich" to "poor" disciplines.

One important manifestation of this egalitarianism is the tendency for teaching loads to be similar across all academic units, regardless of the amount of income they generate from research. If universities were for-profit, hierarchical organizations answerable to stockholders, one would expect each academic unit to specialize according to its potential sources of revenue. Faculty in the humanities, with few opportunities for generating program-based grants and gifts for their research, would specialize in teaching; technical disciplines that could generate substantial revenues from research would allocate less time to educational activities. In practice, teaching loads across disciplines do vary in this fashion. Yet they are still surprisingly equal in research universities, except for medical schools, where many clinical faculty do not teach other than to supervise the medical practice of advanced medical students and interns. The increased research orientation in technical disciplines, driven by the opportunities for external financial support, has thus pulled along other disciplines that have few such opportunities.

The significance of this argument is as follows: universities probably would undertake research regardless of the existence of government and industrial support for it, but they do far more of it than they would if this financial support were unavailable. In addition, the existence of financial support for technical disciplines has increased their relative size and importance within research universities. Were this support to subside, all parts of the university would shrink. These units would shrink more than the others, because their current size is the result of their direct support and the profits that they generate to support other units.

Government policy must take the objectives and behavior of universities into account if it is to induce universities to behave more in accordance with federal goals. Barring the possibility of populating university faculty entirely with altruists, the job of government is to make the objectives and behavior of universities more congruent with those of government by affecting their financial incentives. If government attempts to cut the costs of federally sponsored research in technical disciplines by removing the profits from indirect cost recovery, and to cut federal expenditures for medical care services by eliminating the profits from the operation of university medical centers, universities will respond by withdrawing resources from these activities.

The Causes of Declining State Appropriations

Until the 1990s, the single most important source of revenues for research universities was appropriations from state governments. In fact, until 1990, state appropriations for higher education grew rapidly, frequently at more than 10 percent annually. Starting in 1986, however, the growth in state appropriations slowed appreciably, and state spending has actually fallen in the 1990s.

The effect of the downturn in state spending has been to cause total revenues of all research universities to be roughly constant in inflation-adjusted dollars and the real revenues of public research universities to decline. Figures 2-1 and 2-2 plot annual revenues for both categories of universities, broken down by the categories in table 2-1. As the figures show, all categories of revenues other than state appropriations show similar trends for both types of universities. The only substantial difference between the two figures is in state appropriations, which are extremely important and falling for public universities but insignificant for private ones.

Although other government sources of income for research universities are now also declining, state appropriations were the first to fall and so far have had the biggest and most widespread effect on universities. It is therefore important to understand why this downturn took place. The basic conclusion of our analysis is that the obvious explanations for the downturn only explain a small share of it. As is discussed further, this finding suggests that the prospects for a recovery of state support for research universities are poor.

One potential explanation for declining state support is the change in the age composition of the population. The growing fraction of the population accounted for by elderly people is well known, for it has been widely cited as the factor driving the growth of entitlement programs. The other side of this trend is the declining proportion and number of the population accounted for by college-age adults. Figure 2-3 shows the number of people over age 65 and between the ages of 18 and 24 during the period 1978–93. The end of the postwar baby boom in the 1960s is reflected in the downturn in the number of people between the ages of 18 and 24 that began in 1980.

For two reasons, demographic change does not directly explain the trends in state appropriations for research universities. The slowdown in these revenues did not really begin until the late 1980s, nor the decline in real spending until the 1990s. In addition, as discussed in chapter 3, the decline in the size of the cohort did not signal a drop in enrollments in either all universities and colleges or in research universities in particular.

Of course, state appropriations for research universities are part of a much larger total budget, a growing fraction of which is

Figure 2-1. *Population Cohorts in the United States*

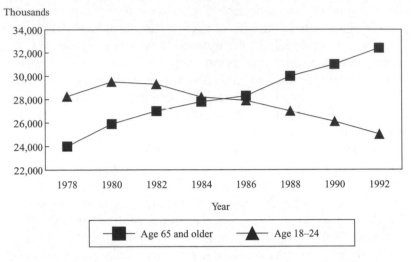

Thousands

Sources: For 1978, Bureau of the Census, *Statistical Abstract of the United States, 1979* (Department of Commerce, 1980), table 30, and for 1979, *Statistical Abstract of Population Estimates: 1980–92*, p. 25–1106 (Department of Commerce, November 1993), table 8, pp. 72–99; and 1991–92, Bureau of the Census, *Current Population Reports: National and State Population Estimates, 1990–94*, pp. 25–1127 (Department of Commerce, July 1995), table 4, pp. 7–13.

devoted to programs for elderly people. Another important source of budgetary pressure on state government has been the extraordinary growth of state correctional institutions. A study of six states with substantial investments in public higher education found that expenditures on prisons had increased substantially and that most of the funds to pay for this growth had come from cuts in higher education.[9] In California, state appropriations for higher education fell from 12.6 percent of the budget in 1980 to 9.5 percent in 1995. Meanwhile, the share of the budget going to prisons grew from 2 percent to 9.9 percent as the prison population climbed from 23,511 to 126,140.[10]

Another important factor affecting the overall state budget, which would affect university appropriations in any state in which higher education claims a large fraction of total expenditures, is the state of the economy. General economic conditions in the United States were disappointing for two decades. The ele-

Figure 2-2. *Sources of Revenues at Private Universities*

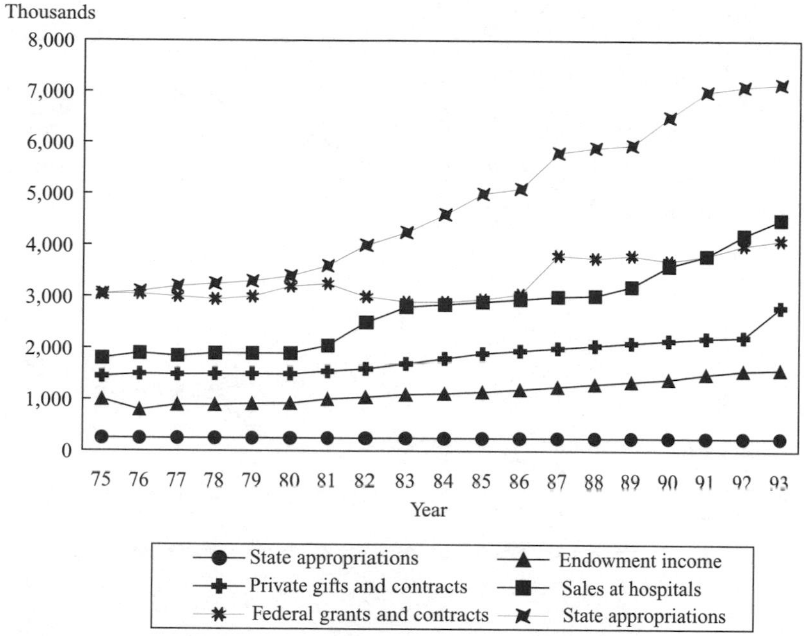

Thousands

Source: National Science Foundation, Computer-Aided Science Policy Anlysis and Research (CASPAR) data file (1997).

ments of this uninspiring economic performance include a slow-down in productivity growth starting in the late 1970s, two serious recessions (including one that was in progress when state appropriations for universities began to decline in the early 1990s), and stagnation or decline in median family income (see chapter 3). In addition, because the hallmark of research universities is training in technical disciplines, a decline in high-technology industries could cause state officials to see less of a need to continue producing graduates in technical disciplines, and so to cut back on expenditures for this purpose. In fact, for the first time in nearly two decades, the number of graduate students in science and engineering declined from 1992 to 1993, although the drop was less than 1 percent.[11] Of course, whether this was the intended purpose of state cutbacks or simply the natural consequence of cuts imposed for other reasons is unclear.

Figure 2-3. *Sources of Revenues at Public Universities*

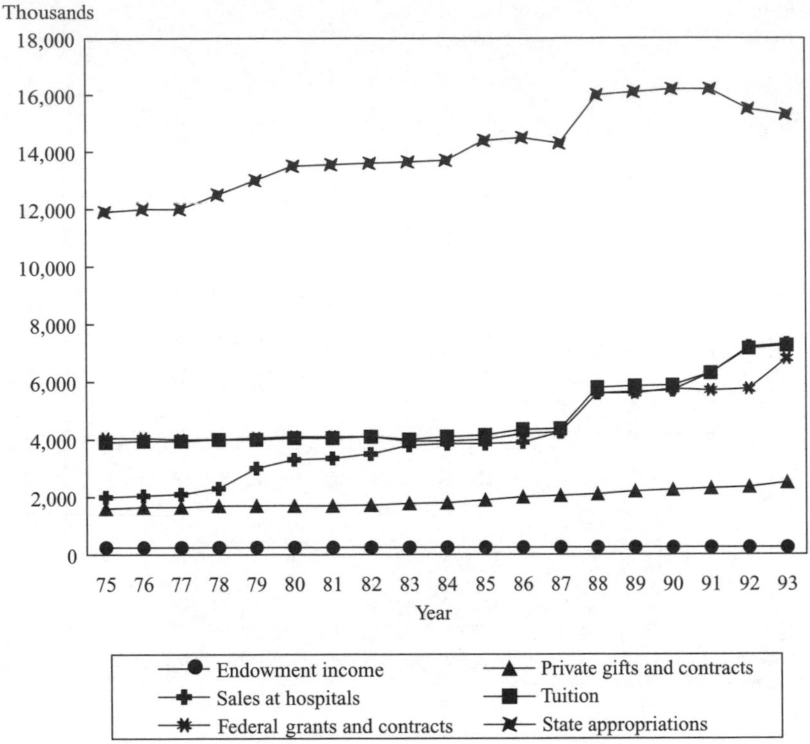

Thousands

Source: National Science Foundation, CASPAR data file.

State budgets reflect political factors as well as economic ones, so one possible explanation for changes in state appropriations is the partisan composition of the government. In particular, the renaissance of the Republican party during the period is generally thought to be associated with growing fiscal conservatism, which may have found expression through state budgets for higher education.

Another factor that might explain trends in state spending is that other sources of revenues may be either substitutes or complements for the objective of most state spending, which is education. Public universities receive relatively little money from industry, so that a strong relationship between industry support and state appropriations is not plausible. Federal grants and hospital revenues are major sources of revenue for public universities; as a result, changes in these revenues could plausibly affect state spending. Of course, these revenues could be substitutes or complements. They are substitutes if states seek to preserve a given level of research and education at public universities, and therefore cut the budgets of research universities if they receive more federal grants and more surplus from university medical centers. These revenues are complements if states invest more funds in universities to enable them to compete more effectively for grants or hospital revenues. Moreover, if state officials perceive that better research and medical centers produce better education, they may shift more resources for higher education into research universities if other sources cause research and medicine to grow.

To test for the importance of these phenomena, we have undertaken an econometric analysis of the factors affecting changes in state appropriations for fiscal years 1980 through 1993. Data for universities come from surveys conducted by the U.S. Department of Education and reported in the Computer-Aided Science Policy Analysis and Research (CASPAR) database system.[12] The universities included in the analysis are the eighty-four public institutions classified as research universities in 1994 by the Carnegie Commission, with the following exceptions. The University of Massachusetts at Amherst is excluded because its data are obviously misreported or misclassified. Rutgers for 1992 and 1993 and Virginia Commonwealth University for 1984–87 are excluded because parts of their data are omitted.

All financial variables in the regression are expressed as the percent change in constant (1987) dollars. The dependent variable in the regression, *State Funds*, is the percentage change in state appropriations for each separate university in each fiscal year. This measure includes state payments for medical services at university medical centers up to 1987 but omits them in subsequent years.

The independent variables are as follows. *Cohort* is the percent change in the number of individuals in the 18- to 24-year-old age cohort within the state at the start of each academic year.[13] *State income* is the percentage change in gross state product, lagged one year to reflect conditions at the time appropriations are made. *Fed grants* is the percentage change in federal grants and contracts to the university in the same fiscal year. This variable is not lagged; grants typically are made several months before the fiscal year begins, so that the amount of awards is reasonably well known in advance. *Governor* measures whether the party identification of the governor changed in the previous calendar year. This variable is 1 if the change was from a Democratic to a Republican administration, –1 if the change was in the opposite direction, and zero otherwise. We focus on the governorship because there was little variation in state legislative control during the sample years. *Hospital (1987)* indicates the percent of university revenues accounted for by hospital sales in 1987. The variable is included to correct for the 1987 accounting change in reported state appropriations.

Total fed R&D is the percentage change in total R&D expenditures by the federal government, and *Net Fed R&D* to *State* is all federal R&D expenditures within the state net of the grants given to the university. *Defense procurement* is the percentage change in federal defense procurement expenditures. These three variables give some indication of overall political support for science and measure the health of high-tech industries (including national laboratories) nationally. The state variable is included to proxy for state high-tech growth. *Year 91–93* is a dummy variable for the years 1991, 1992, and 1993, when state appropriations declined for the first time. These variables are intended to detect whether the underlying politics of public universities changed in this period in ways that cannot be explained by the other causal variables. (Initially we included dummies for each year; however, only those for the last three years were important, and all three had roughly equal coefficients.)

The sample statistics for the variables and the results of the regression are reported in tables 2-4 and 2-5. Three regressions are reported because of multicollinearity between *Defense procurement* and *Year 91–93*.

The overall power of the regression equation, while easily passing tests of statistical significance, is moderate. Each equation explains about half of the mean annual change in state appropriations.

Table 2-4. *Sample Statistics of Regression Variables*

Variable	Mean	Median	Maximum	Minimum	Standard deviation
State funds	0.0154	0.0132	0.332	–0.275	0.072
College cohort	–0.006	–0.008	0.16	–0.057	0.025
State income	0.022	0.022	0.129	–0.161	0.035
Federal grants	0.036	0.03	1.877	–0.694	0.145
Net federal R&D to state	0.035	0.014	24.44	–48.2	1.676
Total federal R&D	0.02	0.006	0.092	–0.034	0.035
Total federal procurement	0.049	0.039	0.19	–0.091	0.088

Source: For state income, 1977–91, *Survey of Current Business* (August 1994), pp. 86–89, table 1; for 1992, *Survey of Current Business* (May 1995), pp. 52–53; for state and federal funds to institutions, National Center for Education Statistics. Institutional data available from CASPAR data file at http://caspar.nsf.gov/webcaspar (1977). For Net federal R&D to states and Total federal R&D, National Science Foundation, *Federal Funds for Research and Department Detailed Historical Tables: Fiscal Years 1956–94*, NSF 94-331 (Bethesda, Md.: Quantum Research Corp. 1994), tables 55, 55a, 55b, and table A; for federal defense procurement, Office of Management and budget, *The Budget for FY 1998, Historical Tables* (Washington), pp. 75–80, table 5–1.

Cohort has the expected sign, but the coefficient is also statistically significantly less than unity, taking values around .35 in all specifications. The value of this coefficient implies that changes in the size of the college-age cohort cause much smaller changes in state appropriations. Most likely, this reflects three phenomena: the growing proportion of the population that attends college and goes on to earn advanced degrees; the tendency for research universities to be more successful than other institutions in retaining their enrollment when the size of the cohort shrinks; and the presence of state objectives for universities other than their educational mission. Because of the inclusion of other variables that vary by year, the coefficient of *Cohort* should be interpreted as reflecting primarily cross-section differences rather than changes over time.[14]

State income is highly significant and positive, indicating that state appropriations rise and fall with the state economy. Although the coefficient is also statistically significantly less than unity, it is nevertheless quite high. This indicates that the percentage change in state appropriations for public research universities is roughly two-thirds of the percentage change in state economic activity.

Table 2-5. *Determinants of State Expenditures on Research Universities*

Standard errors in parentheses

Variable	Equation #1	Equation #2	Equation #3
Constant	−0.0007	0.0012	−0.0081
	[.004]	[.0029]	[.0025]
Cohort	0.35	0.369	0.385
	[.093]	[.091]	[.093]
State income	0.582	0.572	0.581
	[.062]	[.060]	[.062]
Governor	−0.02	−0.02	−0.02
	[.006]	[.006]	[.006]
Fed grants	0.057	0.057	0.056
	[.013]	[.013]	[.013]
Hospital [1987]	−0.235	−0.238	−0.22
	[.056]	[.056]	[.056]
Net fed R&D to state	0.0025	0.0025	0.0026
	[.0011]	[.0011]	[.0011]
Total fed R&D	0.398	0.419	0.445
	[.078]	[.075]	[.077]
Defense procurement	0.025		0.069
	[.029]		[.025]
Year 91–93	−0.0158	−0.0183	
	[.0055]	[.0047]	

Source: Authors' calculations.

Fed grants, too, is positive and statistically significant, indicating a complementarity between state appropriations and federal research grants. The coefficient on this variable is small. Because federal grants and state appropriations are similar in size, the coefficient can be interpreted as implying that a $1 increase in federal grants is associated with an increase in state appropriations of about $0.06. As explained in chapter 4, the effect of federal grants on appropriations is smaller than the fraction of federal grants (roughly 10 percent) that can be interpreted as profits flowing to the general budget of a university. On balance, then, the incremental appropriations to support federal research projects are more than offset by the incremental profit of these activities.

Governor is strongly significant, and the sign is consistent with the hypothesis that Republican conservatism leads to lower budgets for research universities. The results indicate that a change in the political affiliation of the governor changes the appropriations for research universities by about 1 percent.

Hospital is negative and highly significant, but not particularly interesting as it is included as a technical correction. Initially we included a variable indicating changes in the hospital sales at universities with medical schools; however, controlling for the accounting change in 1987, this variable was not significant. These results indicate that hospital expenditures and state appropriations are neither substitutes nor complements. Consequently, if hospital revenues fall by more than hospital costs, these results imply that state appropriations will not respond to make up the difference.

Total fed R&D is also positive and statistically significant, indicating that federal expenditures on research are positively associated with the states' spending on their public research universities. This coefficient measures the average effect on all universities. The magnitude of the coefficient is quite large, indicating that a 10 percent change in federal R&D parallels about a 4 percent change in state appropriations for research universities. Using 1993 financial data, this implies that a $1 million increase in federal R&D leads to an increase of $0.5 million in state appropriations. The implication from this finding is that federal and state objectives and politics are similar, so that other political factors that are not captured in the regression cause both types of appropriations to rise and fall together.

Net fed R&D to state is also positive and significant, although the coefficient on this variable is small. This result indicates that a growing sector of high-tech federal contractors and national labs has a modest positive effect on state appropriations for universities.

The results for *Defense procurement* are equivocal. If *Year 91–93* is not included in the regression, *Defense* is positive and statistically significant. The magnitude of the coefficient implies that a 15 percent cutback in defense procurement would cause a 1 percent reduction in state appropriations. If *Year* is included, *Defense* is statistically insignificant and the coefficient is quite small, although it remains positive.

Finally, the *Year* dummy is highly significant, indicating that the political forces affecting the budgets of research universities have changed in ways not fully accounted for in the regression. The coefficient on this variable is large. In the three years in question, the predicted decline in the rate of growth of state appropriations is about 2.8 percent. From 1980 to 1990, the average percentage increase in state appropriations was 2.3 percent, whereas the mean change after 1990 is –1.2 percent. This difference implies a fall in the average growth rate of 3.5 percentage points. The dummy variable thus accounts for about 80 percent of the slowdown. This result implies that the standard variables that have explained state appropriations for research universities in the past do not account for the recent cutbacks. In particular, most of the recent decline in state support is not due to changes in the college-age population, partisan control of state government, the state of the economy, or federal policy.

The dependence of the significance of *Defense* on whether *Year* is included arises from the correlation between the two. In general, real defense expenditures rose during most of the 1980s but fell during the 1990s. *Year* corresponds roughly to the period when defense expenditures fell. This correlation suggests two possible explanations for the observed statistical results. The significance of *Year* and, when *Year* is excluded, *Defense* might bear no causal relationship to defense procurement, in which case the corresponding decline in employment opportunities in technical disciplines was not a factor in state budget decisions for research universities. In addition, the actual relationship between state appropriations and *Defense* may differ depending on whether *Defense* is growing or falling, with cuts in the defense procurement budget having a greater effect than increases. The latter possibility is not implausible. Before the end of the cold war, states could have interpreted annual variations in the defense budget as reflecting short-term changes in the economy and the ideological composition of the federal government against a backdrop of a defense sector that, in the long run, was likely to remain roughly stable. However, the end of the cold war has been widely interpreted as signaling a long-term change in the size of the defense sector and the large number of defense jobs that require higher education in engineering or science.

Conclusions

In this chapter we have explored the financial incentives facing research universities and their implications for the structure of these institutions. The data on revenue sources reveal that a fundamental change is taking place in the incentives facing research universities. In general, government support is becoming less important, while support from private parties through tuition, donations, grants, and sales of nonmedical services is becoming more so. This change implies that research universities are likely to put less emphasis on serving the public policy goals of government and more on attracting tuition payments from students and payments from businesses for research and services.

The implications of these changes for university medical schools, which are explored in detail in chapter 6, are especially significant. Just as research universities responded to the rapid growth in health care expenditures in the 1970s and 1980s by greatly expanding their provision of health care through university medical centers, they are likely to respond to the end of this boom—and the new focus on cost containment, which disproportionately affects the relatively expensive care that universities provide—by withdrawing from this activity.

The trends in state expenditures indicate that a fundamental change has taken place in the political support for research universities, a change that does not bode well for these institutions. The decline in state support does not reflect changes in the traditional factors that have explained state appropriations in the past. States did not cut back solely in response to current economic changes and changes in the college-age cohort—the cutbacks were far too large to be explained by these factors. Of course, state appropriations still are the most important source of support for public universities. But the fraction of the revenues of public research universities that is accounted for by state appropriations has fallen precipitously, from around 40 percent in the 1970s and early 1980s to less than 30 percent by 1993. About three-quarters of the decline in the importance of state appropriations was accounted for by huge increases in sales of medical services; however, this revenue stream is now declining as well.

The likely effect of such declines is that public universities will grow to resemble private universities as they rely more and more on tuition, private grants, and donations as sources of revenues. The implication of these changes is that public research universities are likely to place less emphasis on providing educational opportunities for students from low- and middle-income families and on engaging in other public service activities.

Endnotes

1. For an earlier study with a similar approach but a different emphasis, see Michael S. McPherson, Morton Owen Schapiro, and Gordon C. Winston, *Paying the Piper: Productivity, Incentives, and Financing in U.S. Higher Education* (University of Michigan Press, 1993).

2. A list of the Carnegie Classification Research I and Research II universities can be found at http://cause-www.colorado.edu/member-dir/institutions_by_carnegie.html. Table 2-1 includes schools identified by the NSF-Caspar data base.

3. In fiscal 1994, state governments appropriated $41.2 billion for higher education, and local governments appropriated $4.4 billion. Of these amounts, $39.8 and $4.0 billion, respectively, went to public institutions. Public research universities received $14.6 billion from state government, but only $0.2 billion from local government, while private research universities received $0.4 billion from the states and $0.2 billion from locals. See Department of Education, *Digest of Educational Statistics, 1995*, table 322.

4. "Sources of Voluntary Support for Higher Education, 1994–1995," *Chronicle of Higher Education Almanac*, September 2, 1996, p. 27. This accounting apparently includes donations to endowment funds (omitted from the accounts in table 2-1) and may not include all contract funds.

5. Some schools report physician practice plan income in the "Sales of Educational Activities" category, and others include such income in the hospital accounts. The former practice is fairly common, as universities with medical schools report, on average, at least twice the share of

revenues from sales of educational activities as those without, and the discrepancy has grown over time. In 1975, private universities without medical schools reported an average of 1.2 percent of revenues in this category, and those with medical schools reported 2.8 percent. Public universities without medical schools reported 1.75 percent on average, and those with medical schools reported 2.7 percent of revenues in this category. In 1993 the respective statistics for private universities were 1.4 percent and 5.5 percent and for public universities, 2.9 percent and 4.8 percent. National Science Foundation, Computer-Aided Science Policy Analysis and Research (CASPAR) data file.

6. National Science Foundation, *Academic Science and Engineering: R&D Expenditures*, NSF Doc. 96-308 (Arlington, Va., 1996), pp. 74–75.

7. Almost all federal R&D expenditures at colleges and universities are accounted for by the Carnegie research universities plus other medical schools. According to the National Science Foundation, the top 150 universities (which include nineteen medical schools that are not part of research universities plus the Woods Hole Research Institute), accounted for more than 90 percent of all R&D expenditures by universities and colleges. Ibid., pp. 25, 74–76.

8. For fiscal 1993, the federal government provided nearly $20 billion in academic R&D, distributed as follows:

Life sciences	$10.8 billion
Medical sciences	5.3 billion
Biological sciences	3.5 billion
Agricultural sciences	1.6 billion
Other	0.4 billion
Engineering	3.2 billion
Physical sciences	2.1 billion
Environmental sciences	1.3 billion
Social sciences	0.9 billion
Computer sciences	0.6 billion
Psychology	0.3 billion
Mathematics	0.3 billion

National Science Board, *Science & Engineering Indicators–1996*, NSB 96-21 (Government Printing Office, 1996), appendix table 5-6, p. 173.

9. Steven D. Gold, ed., *The Fiscal Crisis of the States: Lessons for the Future* (Georgetown University Press, 1995). The states are California, Connecticut, Florida, Massachusetts, Michigan, and Minnesota.

10. *New York Times* (national edition), April 12, 1995, p. A11.

11. National Science Foundation, *Data Brief* (Arlington, Va., July 24, 1996).

12. This data set is available at the National Science Foundation web site: http://www.qrc.com/nsf/srs/caspar/start.htm.

13. There are some shifts in 1980 and 1990 in some of the smaller states that seem unlikely and are probably because data for those years are based on a census and the intermediate years on extrapolations. However, the regressions were not affected by omitting the suspicious observations.

14. When the *Year* and *Fed R&D* variables are omitted, the *Cohort* variable turns insignificant. Alternatively, when dummies are included for each year, the coefficient is robust. This suggests that states with unusual increases (decreases) in the college-age cohort were more (less) willing to support state universities than other states in the same year.

Chapter 3

Students and Research Universities

Gary Burtless and Roger G. Noll

In this chapter we review evidence on the value to students of receiving higher education at a research university. Remarkably little research has addressed this issue. Almost all research on the relationship between universities and students fails to distinguish between types of universities. This chapter briefly reviews the data on tuition costs and the evidence about the earnings premium to higher education and summarizes the sparse information available about research universities.

College Costs

Among parents of college-bound students, it is notorious that tuition increases substantially outpaced general inflation during the 1980s and early 1990s. Between 1980 and 1994, annual tuition costs (in constant 1994 dollars) roughly doubled, from $6,000 to $12,000, for private four-year colleges, and increased by about 60 percent, from about $1,500 to $2,400, for public four-year colleges.[1]

Tuition is not the only component of the sticker price of college, but other costs have risen more in line with general inflation. Between 1980 and 1992, the total average sticker price of college attendance in constant 1992 dollars rose from $9,069 to $14,514 (60 percent) for four-year private colleges, and from $4,134 to $5,936 (44 percent) for four-year public colleges.[2]

Of course, students do not necessarily pay these prices, because various forms of financial aid are offered to some of them. Average student aid did increase during this period, rising from $3,086 to $3,256 (6 percent), but this change was much smaller than the increase in costs.[3] For middle-income families the ability to pay did not increase much. The 1980s saw little growth in incomes for most Americans (a point to be examined in some detail), as median family income rose from $35,839 to $36,812.[4] The sum of the increase in financial aid plus family income, then, was less than the increase in the sticker price of college attendance for both private and public institutions.

These data suggest that college attendance became more difficult to finance for most prospective students. A natural expectation from a situation such as this, with prices increasing more rapidly than income, is a drop in sales—in this case, a reduced rate of college attendance. In fact, precisely the opposite occurred.[5] Enrollment in U.S. higher education actually increased from 12.2 million in 1980 to 14.5 million in 1991, while the total population in the 20- to 24–year-old cohort declined from 21.6 million to 19.0 million. As a result, from 1980 to 1991, the proportion of 24–year-olds holding a first university degree climbed from 21.8 percent to 29.2 percent.

These data create something of a puzzle. If college became less affordable to Americans, why were more students enrolling and remaining in college long enough to earn a degree? An economist's answer is that despite the higher price, the value of a college education increased enough so that college attendance became more, not less, attractive. College can be more attractive either because the wages of college-educated people are rising (even though incomes in general are not), or because the alternatives to college are getting worse. In fact, both effects appear to have been at work in the 1980s.

The Earnings Premium to Higher Education

Higher education serves many purposes. It can certainly be an enjoyable experience for students, regardless of any economic

benefits it confers. Nevertheless, an underlying economic rationale for education is that it produces "human capital." In other
words, education is an investment that enhances the future earning potential of the student.[6]

Americans have traditionally valued higher education as an
investment in their children's future, and their faith has not been
misplaced. Figures 3-1 to 3-4 display basic information about the
returns to higher education for men and women since 1969. Figures 3-1 (for men) and 3-2 (for women) show the ratio of the
median earnings of workers who have college degrees to the
median earnings of high school graduates who did not attend
college. Both men and women obtain roughly the same percentage earnings premium from a college degree. In 1993, men and
women with four years of college earned 60 percent more than
high school graduates, and those with five or more years of college earned more than twice as much as high school graduates.

Figures 3-3 and 3-4 show actual earnings in constant 1993
dollars among full-time workers with differing levels of school
attainment. From these figures we can calculate the exact earnings
premium for different levels of educational attainment. In 1993,
four years of college produced an annual earnings premium over
a high school degree of approximately $15,000 for men and
$11,000 for women. More university education boosted the an-
nual earnings premium by an additional $13,000 for men and
$9,000 for women.

Figures on actual earnings reveal other important trends in
the earnings premium for educational attainment. For both men
and women the earnings premium from four years of college
declined in the 1970s, then rose dramatically after 1980. For additional years of college, the earnings premium remained roughly
unchanged for both men and women in the 1970s and then rose
for both sexes in the 1980s. In addition, real earnings for workers
who did not attend college have declined since 1979 and have
shrunk even for men who attended but did not complete college.
By contrast, real earnings for workers with four years of college
have risen sharply for women and slightly for men. Among men,
the only group that has enjoyed sizable earnings gains consists of
workers with more than four years of college.

Figure 3-1. *Earnings Premium of Male College Graduates, 1969–93*

Percent of high school graduates' median wage

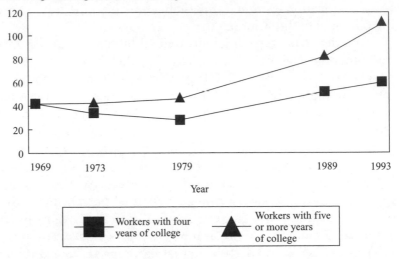

Year

Source: Authors' estimates using March Current Population Survey files.
Note: The earnings premium is calculated as the difference between college graduates' and high-school graduates median annual earnings, measured as a percentage of high-school graduates' median earnings. Median earnings are estimated based on data for full-time, year-round wage and salary workers.

An important factor in the recent surge in the college earnings premium is the absolute decline in real earnings among workers who have not attended college, as shown in figures 3-3 and 3-4. A second important factor is the increase in the real income of college-educated women, which has reduced the gender gap in earnings by about 20 percent. The last factor, increases in real earnings, is significant only for women with four or more years of college and for men with five or more years.

These data imply that the returns to higher education are substantial. Using the information on college costs and earnings by educational status, we can estimate the returns to higher education. For example, a woman who pays the average cost of private education, net of financial aid, for four years of college will spend about $45,000.[7] In addition, while in college she will have to forego about 75 percent of the earnings of a female high school graduate, which amounts to approximately $50,000 over

Figure 3-2. *Earnings Premium of Female College Graduates, 1969–93*

Percent of high school graduate's median wage

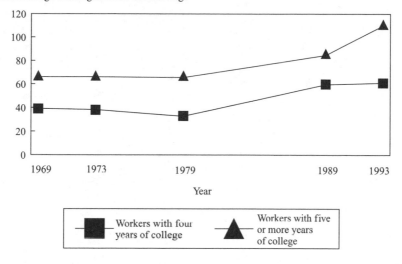

Year

Source: Authors' estimates using March Current Population Survey files.
Note: The earnings premium is calculated as the difference between college graduates' and high-school graduates median annual earnings, measured as a percentage of high-school graduates' median earnings. Median earnings are estimated based on data for full-time, year-round wage and salary workers.

four years. This is the opportunity cost of attending college rather than working. Adding together the direct cost and the opportunity cost, higher education requires a total investment of about $95,000.[8] The benefit is the $11,000 earnings premium a woman can expect to receive as a full-time worker. For women who anticipate working full time over a twenty-five-year career, this benefit yields a return on her investment amounting to about 12.5 percent per year. Similar calculations suggest that a man will sacrifice approximately $80,000 in forgone earnings plus $45,000 in net tuition to obtain $15,000 in additional annual earnings, yielding a 14 percent return. For both men and women, then, the return on investment for a college education is substantially higher than they are likely to receive from any other investment.

Viewed another way, these data are not as encouraging. Because for many years the real cost of college net tuition, after subtracting financial aid subsidies, has been rising faster than the

Figure 3-3. *Median Earnings for Male Workers by Educational Attainment, 1969–93*

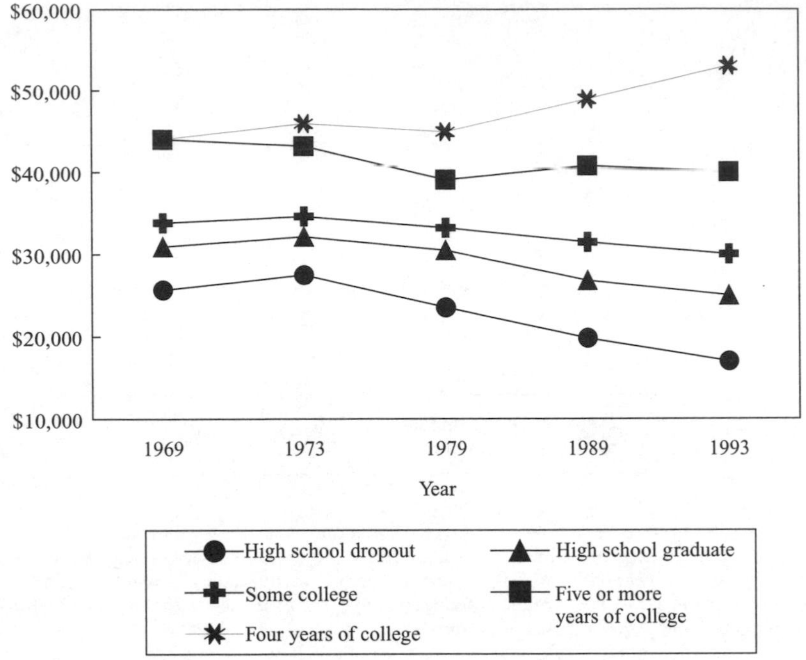

Source: Authors' estimates using March Current Population Survey files.

real earnings of college graduates, the ratio of college costs to the earnings of a college graduate has risen substantially. Nevertheless, the forgone earnings of a high school graduate are a more important source of college costs for all students except those who attend the most expensive private institutions. Because the real earnings of high-school graduates have fallen, this component of the cost of college has fallen as well. For example, the real annual earnings of male high school graduates fell nearly $5,000 between 1979 and 1993. If the foregone earnings of a college student are 75 percent of the earnings of a high-school graduate, the annual lost earnings from attending college rather than working dropped by about $3,500 between 1979 and 1993. Because this amount is substantially larger than the increase in the total average cost of a four-year public college, these institutions actually became

Figure 3-4. *Median Earnings for Female Workers by Educational Attainment, 1969–93*

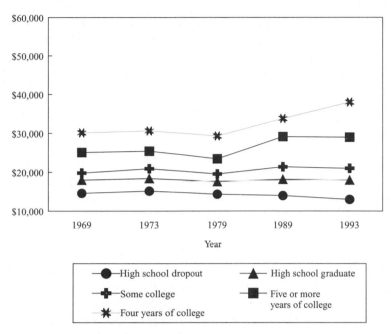

Source: Authors' estimates using March Current Population Survey files.

cheaper during the 1980s, despite the rapid increase in tuition. For four-year private colleges, the increase in the average cost of college was greater than the reduction in the earnings sacrifice of men, so that private colleges did become more expensive, but not by nearly as much as the increase in tuition.

For women, the story is different. Earnings of female high school graduates have risen, though by very little. But real annual earnings of female college graduates have risen by about $6,000. As a result, for women college has become more expensive, but the earnings benefits derived from attending have roughly doubled.

These crude data provide an important insight into the puzzle of growing enrollments in the face of rising prices. Despite rising prices, the college earnings premium has increased. For men, the cause is a drop in their forgone earnings, due to the drop in annual income of high school graduates. For women, the cause is a sharp increase in the earnings of college graduates.

Because the federal government concentrates its support for research and education in fields of natural science and engineering, another relevant indicator is the relative earnings of students in these fields. Recent survey data from the National Science Foundation confirm that graduates with natural science and engineering degrees earn more than other students. For example, the median salary in 1995 of students who graduated in 1993 and 1994 with a degree in social sciences was $21,000 for bachelor's degrees and $30,000 for master's degrees. By contrast, the median salary for engineers was $33,500 for bachelor's degrees and $44,000 for master's degrees. Wages in all fields of natural science were also higher than in the social sciences, although the figures for degrees in life sciences were only slightly higher.[9]

These numbers do not prove conclusively that college is the *cause* of higher income, of course. College graduates might possess greater intelligence or other attributes that employers value, implying that college attendance does not actually cause the earnings premium. A great deal of economic research has addressed this issue. Virtually all economists conclude that, even correcting for personal attributes, a college education does indeed enhance earnings substantially. Surprisingly, one recent survey of this literature concluded that the correlation between educational attainment and student endowments (such as intelligence, other personal traits, and the quality of elementary and secondary education) is sufficiently complex that the direction of the bias in simply using raw earnings statistics (as was done here) to measure the benefits of higher education remains ambiguous![10] The most comprehensive survey of research on the returns to higher education reviewed forty-three studies. It found that the mean estimate of the real rate of return was 12 percent, which is reasonably close to the simple estimates presented in this section.[11]

The Special Case of Research Universities

For the purposes of this book, an important shortcoming of nearly all existing research on the economic value of college education is that it focuses on the returns to higher education in general rather than higher education received at research universities. As discussed in chapter 1, the key issue in evaluating educational aspects of research universities is whether education and research are complementary. In principle, integrating teaching and research has three potentially important payoffs for education.

First, success in research, as revealed by success in obtaining peer-reviewed grants and publishing peer-reviewed books and journal articles, may indicate that the researcher is at the frontier of some field of knowledge. A person who is not engaged in research is not likely to be at the forefront of knowledge, if for no other reason than the delays in disseminating research results. To the extent that the quality of education depends on the currency of the information transmitted, institutions of higher education that encourage and support research therefore have an advantage over those that do not produce research. Moreover, if "learning by doing" plays a role in the acquisition of technical knowledge, people who do research will have an additional advantage as teachers over those who do not.

In addition, education in technical fields may be more effective if students are able to learn by doing through participation in faculty research activities. In the laboratory sciences, effectiveness in research requires the development of practical skills in laboratory techniques, and in many fields computers play an important role in research. Any educational institution can involve students in research projects that develop laboratory and computer skills. But a research university, by virtue of its more extensive research activities, can offer richer opportunities. This argument lies at the heart of the concern in European countries that university education in science and engineering is too theoretical and not sufficiently practical.[12]

Finally, education and research might exhibit economies of scope—that is, they might be produced more cheaply together than they could be produced separately. These economies may be real, in that joint use of facilities and people for education and research is more efficient. Or they might be purely financial in that research universities, as nonprofit institutions, pass on some of their "profits" from research to students in the form of lower prices or higher quality.

Little research has attempted to measure whether research universities produce a greater return on investment than other institutions of higher education. Moreover, only one of these studies has been published since the 1970s![13] The main finding from these studies is that the quality of a university is positively correlated with the earnings of college graduates. However, the measured size of these effects varies dramatically across studies, largely because the studies differ in the extent to which they control for other factors affecting earnings outcomes.

The most comprehensive study to date—one conducted by Behrman, Rosenzweig, and Taubman—focuses on identical female twins from Minnesota who were born between 1936 and 1955.[14] By studying identical twins from a state that is relatively homogeneous ethnically, these researchers were able to hold constant all of the differences among students that arise from family characteristics, precollege education, and (arguably) genetic endowment. Behrman and colleagues use characteristics of the university attended, as well as the amount of education received, to measure the effect of the quality of a university.

For our purposes, the relevant measures of university quality are total university expenditures per student (a measure of research intensity as well as inputs to education), the ratio of students to faculty (which, among universities, is lower if many faculty are engaged extensively in research), whether the university grants a doctoral degree (which is largely overlapping with whether an institution is a research university), and the average salary of a full professor (which also is generally higher in research universities). In their most comprehensive model, Behrman and colleagues find that all measures associated with research universities have a significantly positive effect on earnings: earnings are higher for graduates of Ph.D. institutions with high expenditures per pupil, high average professorial salaries, and low student-teacher ratios.[15] Moreover, these effects are quantitatively quite large. For example, if other effects are held constant, identical twins who attended Ph.D. institutions earned 50 percent more; those who attended universities that spend twice as much per student earned 83 percent more.

A second approach to measuring the effect of research universities on the net benefits of education is to examine whether increased income for research benefits students through lower tuition charges or greater financial aid. McPherson and Schapiro collected financial information on nearly 2,000 colleges and universities. They constructed a model of university finances that enabled them to trace the effects of changes in research support.[16] Their findings are reported in table 3-1. One should be wary of these findings, partly because government data on the financial operations of universities are notoriously unreliable, and partly because one would like to have enough solid data to take into account more factors that influence university budget allocations. Nevertheless, the study is carefully done and is the best yet undertaken on this issue. The results indicate that the effect of research is to reduce tuition, increase financial aid, and raise expenditures on instruction. These findings suggest that research and education are complements, not substitutes.

The conclusion that research universities add more value to their students is therefore supported by the available fragmentary evidence. College in general commands a wage premium; wages are generally higher in natural science and engineering, which receive most federal support and in which research universities play a more prominent role. The indicators used to identify research universities are strongly positively correlated with the earnings of college graduates, holding constant other factors that affect earnings. In addition, financial information about university budgeting indicates that research and education are cost complements: more money for research means lower net tuition prices and higher expenditures on education. Nevertheless, the available research on this issue is not very extensive, suggesting that more work needs to be done to quantify accurately the value to students of attending research universities.

Education of Foreigners

An indirect indicator of the quality and value of American higher education is the number of foreign students who attend

Table 3-1. *Effects on Students of One U.S. Dollar in Federal Research Grants*

	Institution	
Budget item	Four-year private	Four-year public
Instruction	+$.22	+$.13
Tuition and fees	−$.22	−$.10
Financial aid	+$.11	+$.04

Source: Michael S. McPherson and Morton Owen Schapiro, "The Effect of Government Financing on the Behavior of Colleges and Universities," in Michael S. McPherson, Morton Owen Schapiro, and Gordon C. Winston, *Paying the Piper: Productivity, Incentives, and Financing in U.S. Higher Education* (University of Michigan Press, 1993), p. 248.

U.S. colleges and universities. American higher education attracts many foreign students, especially in graduate programs that are dominated by research universities. These students are very likely to remain in the United States, and they now account for an impressive share of total employment in research and higher education. To the extent that U.S. economic growth depends on higher education and research, the role of universities in attracting foreign students is an important benefit to the U.S. economy. This section reviews the education and postgraduate activities of foreign students.

During the second half of the twentieth century, the number of foreign students enrolled in higher education in the United States grew enormously. In 1955 fewer than 40,000 foreigners were enrolled in U.S. universities and colleges, but by 1990 their number had grown to nearly 400,000.[17] The most important source of foreign students has always been Asia, but the dominance of Asia has grown substantially. By 1990 Asian students represented about 60 percent of all foreign students, up from 40 percent in the 1950s, and the top five nations in supplying foreign students were China, Japan, Taiwan, India, and Korea.[18]

The importance of research universities in attracting foreign students arises from the concentration of foreigners in graduate studies and in science and engineering. Over half of foreign students are enrolled in science, engineering, or health fields, and nearly half are graduate students.[19] Whereas nonresident foreign students—that is, foreign-born students who are neither naturalized citizens nor permanent resident aliens—account for only about three percent of undergraduates in the United States, they receive about twelve percent of all master's degrees and 25 percent of all doctorates.[20] The number of noncitizens enrolled in undergraduate programs has fallen by about 6 percent since its 1983 peak, but the number of noncitizen graduate students continued to increase until 1994.[21]

The concentration of foreigners in more technical disciplines is shown in table 3-2, which contains the number of degrees awarded in 1993 to all students and to nonresident aliens by area of study. The table shows that about 30 percent of foreign undergraduate degrees are in natural science or engineering, compared with about 15 percent for all students. At the graduate level, about 15 percent of all master's degrees and 45 percent of all doctorates are in natural science or engineering, whereas among foreign students 40 percent of master's degrees and two-thirds of doctorates are in these fields.

As a result of this concentration of foreign students in advanced study in technical disciplines, foreign students have become an extremely important component of graduate education in the United States. As can can be seen table 3-2, about a quarter of all master's degrees and a third of all doctorates in science and engineering are earned by foreign students. In every field of science and engineering except psychology, foreign students account for more than one-quarter of all doctorates, and in engineering foreigners earn over half of the degrees.[22]

The preceding data actually understate the importance of foreign-born students in American higher education because many of the data distinguish only between citizens and noncitizens, or between permanent and temporary residents. Of course, foreigners can arrive with a permanent visa and then earn citizenship while attending school, or they can arrive as temporary residents but earn permanent status before they earn a degree. Some of the data series stop measuring these students as foreign when they change immigration status.

Changes in status during schooling increased due to two policy changes in the 1990s. The Immigration Act of 1990 changed procedures for granting permanent visas by giving higher prior-

Table 3-2. *Number of Degrees by Field, 1993*
Thousands

	Bachelor's		Master's		Doctorate	
Field	Total	Nonresident aliens	Total	Nonresident aliens	Total	Nonresident aliens
All[a]	1,179	32	371	44	40	10
Engineering	63	5	28	9	6	3
Natural science	117	5	28	8	13	4
Social science	209	4	26	3	7	1
Other	791	19	290	24	14	2

Source: National Science Foundation, *Science and Engineering Degrees by Race/Ethnicity of Recipients 1985–93*, NSF 95-330 (Arlington, Va., 1995), pp. 46, 48, 58, 60, 70, 72.
a. Columns may not add due to rounding.

ity to highly skilled individuals and their family members.[23] Because the children of highly educated people are more likely to attend college, this change probably increased the number of foreign-born students who are permanent residents and naturalized citizens and may have encouraged immigration specifically for the purpose of attending U.S. universities. Then, in the wake of Tiananmen Square, the Chinese Student Protection Act of 1992 allowed Chinese nationals with temporary visas to change their status to permanent residents, allowing 26,915 Chinese to adjust their status.[24]

Regardless of their immigration status and their motives for attending American universities, foreign students are very likely to remain in the United States. A survey of students who received doctorates in 1995 revealed that among students who have made decisions about postgraduate employment, most planned to remain in the United States.[25] Among U.S. citizens, only 628 of the 18,065 students with firm plans accepted a position in a foreign country. Of the 2,073 foreigners with permanent visas who had made post-graduation plans, only 172 intended to go abroad. For the 4,699 doctoral students with temporary visas, 2,173 planned to leave the country, but 2,491 had decided to stay in the United States despite their "temporary" status.

Employment data bear out the significance of foreign-born scientists and engineers in the economy. In 1993 total U.S. employment of scientists and engineers with doctorates was 462,870, and of these 81.5 percent were native-born U.S. citizens.[26] Only 61.4 percent of those with doctorates employed as engineers were native U.S. citizens. Table 3-3 contains the distribution of the employment of Ph.D. holders by sector of the economy, and even in the federal government native citizens account for less than 90 percent of employment.

The role of research universities in the overall immigration process is substantial. Research universities play a dominant role in educating foreign students because foreign students are atypically likely to be graduate students in technical disciplines, and most of these students stay in the United States. Students may come to the United States because they believe an American education is superior or because they believe that geographic proximity will facilitate a job search in the United States. In either case, universities facilitate immigration of highly educated workers in technical disciplines.

The desirability of immigration is always a controversial issue in American politics. Some believe that the United States should not admit so many foreigners, even if they are scientists and engineers seeking advanced degrees. Two arguments against admitting foreign students are as follows. One is that those who stay suppress wages and block career advancement of native citizens or even displace them. The other is that those who do not stay cause their home nations to be more effective international competitors against U.S. industry.

Both arguments have a germ of truth but are incomplete and misleading assessments of the effect of educating foreigners. Students who remain in the United States do increase the supply of well-educated people and so probably reduce their wages. But as demonstrated elsewhere in this chapter, the earnings premium attributable to education has increased, not diminished, during the period in which foreign enrollments in American higher education have increased.

Table 3-4 shows the median salaries of holders of doctorates by field of doctorate and immigration status. These data reveal a

Table 3-3. *Percentage Distribution of Employment of Ph.D.s by Immigration Status, 1993*

	Sector of Employment							
Status	Higher education	Other education	Business	Self-employed	Nonprofit	Federal government	State/local government	Other
U.S. native	82.0	87.9	76.2	89.2	84.8	89.0	85.2	48.9
Naturalized citizen	8.8	7.3	14.1	7.5	9.1	9.3	9.8	7.2
Permanent visa	6.7	4.0	7.8	2.9	4.4	1.0	4.3	15.8
Temporary visa	2.4	0.8	1.9	0.4	1.6	0.6	0.5	23.7

Source: National Science Foundation, *Characteristics of Doctoral Scientists and Engineers in the United States: 1993*, NSF 96-302 (Arlington, Va., 1993), p. 51.

strong correlation between the immigration status of foreigners and their wages. Workers with temporary visas earn far less than other doctorate holders; however, temporary visa holders are dominated by postdoctoral students, who are just beginning their careers. Temporary residents can qualify for this type of employment (which otherwise is usually barred for holders of temporary visas) because it is regarded as a continuation of education. Foreigners with permanent visas earn substantially more than temporary residents, but less than naturalized citizens. These differences also are likely to reflect age and career stage because some immigrants with permanent visas eventually qualify and apply for citizenship.

Finally, naturalized citizens earn somewhat more than native citizens. Again, this difference mostly reflects age effects. The wages of native citizens span the full career ladder, whereas many naturalized citizens are classified as temporary or permanent noncitizen residents during their early careers. This conclusion is supported by comparison of native citizens and all foreigners. The median salary for all employees with doctorates exceeds or equals the median for native U.S. citizens. These data are inconsistent with the view that employers can successfully discriminate against immigrant scientists and engineers and that low-wage foreigners are displacing high-wage Americans.

Table 3-4. *Median Salaries of Science and Engineering Ph.D.s by Field and Immigration Status, 1993*

		Field of doctorate				
Status	All	Computer and mathematics	Life sciences	Physical sciences	Social sciences	Engineering
All	$60,400	$60,200	$55,600	$65,700	$52,400	$72,000
U.S. native	60,100	60,100	55,200	65,500	52,400	72,100
Naturalized citizen	65,600	60,500	60,300	67,400	51,600	71,300
Permanent visa	52,500	51,400	47,500	51,300	46,500	58,500
Temporary visa	40,200	40,100	31,300	35,600	43,500	47,600

Source: National Science Foundation, *Characteristics of Doctoral Scientists and Engineers in the United States: 1993*, NSF 96-302 (Arlington, Va., 1996), p. 89.

Because foreign students are so heavily concentrated in technical disciplines, the jobs they hold are more likely to be in research, which provides substantial spillover benefits. To the extent that the social returns to research exceed the private returns to those who undertake it, researchers will be paid wages that fall below their incremental contribution to national income. Hence foreign students who stay in the United States to engage in research are creating a net social benefit for other Americans.

Recently some scholars have argued that the United States is overinvesting in graduate education and that a simple solution is to reduce the education of foreign students. A prominently mentioned example is a study by Massey and Goldman, projecting a large future excess supply of doctorates in science and engineering in the United States.[27] These studies argue that the demand for scientists and engineers is stagnant, that many doctorate holders are not engaged in research and therefore are overeducated, and that in any case wages will not adjust to balance supply and demand. If, as seems likely, these studies are correct in assuming that employment for researchers in universities and government laboratories is likely to fall, the key to these forecasts is the belief that much employment of doctorate holders elsewhere does not make use of their education, and that many doctorate holders could hold the same jobs with only a master's degree.

A major problem with this argument is that the evidence indicates that holders of science and engineering doctorates are not suffering. The income data in table 3-4 show that the earnings of foreign scientists and engineers are far above those of the other educational groups examined in this chapter. In addition, doctorate holders have an unemployment rate of less than two percent, and in 1993, in the midst of the national debate about corporate downsizing and job demotions among the middle class, only 4.3 percent were involuntarily employed outside of their field of specialization.[28]

The conclusion that many Ph.D. holders are overeducated rests on the assumption that a doctorate is a useful degree only if the holder works in advanced research, which takes place primarily in academia and government labs. This perspective seems to reflect the values of academics, who may well evaluate their success as graduate educators on the basis of placing students in these positions. The appropriate perspective is that of the Ph.D. students who hold other types of positions.

For academic scientists and engineers to argue that policymakers should restrict graduate enrollments is perilously close to a narrowly self-serving argument to limit competition and to elevate wages by creating a shortage. The essence of this recommendation is that highly educated undergraduates who qualify for advanced training in technical disciplines should be denied the opportunity to further their education against their wishes. According to employment and earnings data, such a policy would force prospective graduate students to accept jobs that pay less than positions as Ph.D.-holding scientists and engineers, not to mention making them abandon their careers of choice. Most likely this policy would lead to higher wages for those who already have doctorates. But it is not at all clear why society should want to pursue this objective, especially when the occupations that employ doctorates—education and research—are atypically prone to create spillover benefits that accrue to society generally, rather than solely to employees and employers in higher wages and profits.

Students who return home may also contribute to education and research abroad, thereby causing higher productivity in their home economies. By far the most important effect of their return migration is an increase in overall economic growth throughout the world. The United States is benefited, not harmed, by improved economic performance in other countries. Rising production elsewhere primarily increases income and consumption in the country where it occurs. Moreover, rising income elsewhere increases the demand for U.S. products as much as it substitutes for domestic production, and this process improves the economic welfare of consumers everywhere.

Beyond their larger economic significance, the attacks on the appropriateness of educating foreign students have profound consequences for American research universities. Because foreign students are a substantial fraction of graduate enrollments, the scope and quality of research universities would be profoundly affected by a policy that curtailed these enrollments. Recall that the evidence indicates that, contrary to common belief, research and education are complementary, rather than substitutes. Foreign students play an important role in university research, and students on foreign fellowships, through their tuition payments, help defray the fixed costs of education. A significant reduction in the enrollment of foreign students would reduce the quality of research universities by reducing both contributions.

Conclusions

The key question in assessing the educational role of research universities is whether they are worth the price. Unfortunately, too little research has focused on this question, so the issue cannot be definitively resolved. The key point is that attending a research university is privately worthwhile if it provides a good return on the student's investment. The data strongly suggest that this is the case. Education and research appear to be complements: each increases the productivity and reduces the cost of the other. A large number of foreign students are attracted to the United States for graduate study, and they have come to account for a significant fraction of graduate students in technical disciplines. Most of these students remain in the United States and have essentially the same employment and earnings experiences as native-born citizens.

A broader conclusion about higher education is also implied by the data. The human capital approach views education as a crucial input that helps determine the lifetime productivity of a student. Changes in the sticker price of higher education are not the appropriate measure of the change in its true cost. The measure of cost must also include the earnings students give up in order to attend college. Because the earnings of workers without any college education have shrunk in recent years, one important component of the cost of college has actually declined. Even more important, the key determinant of the long-term value of a college education—the college earnings premium—has risen sharply since 1980. Despite steep increases in the sticker price of college and stagnation in financial aid, college attendance is a better deal for most students today than it was in the 1960s and 1970s.

The rising earnings premium attributable to higher education took place in an era of rising enrollment of foreign students in the highly rewarding fields of science and engineering. Foreign-born employees account for nearly a fifth of scientists and engineers with doctorates and so play a substantial role in research-intensive industries. Thus both research universities and high-tech companies would be significantly harmed by policy actions to curtail enrollment by foreign students.

The implication of this analysis for research universities is most assuredly not that rising tuition will stop being a controversial issue. But these findings do suggest that the demand for educational services is one area in which strong institutions can expect to experience solid and even growing demand. The size of the 20- to 24-year-old cohort in the United States will remain at about 18 million until 2002 and then begin to increase. If the earnings premium on higher education continues to grow, high school graduates in the next decade, like those in the 1980s and 1990s, will want to attend college, even at historically high tuition prices. In addition, in the absence of short-sighted policies to keep out foreigners, the strength of U.S. universities plus a strong U.S.

economy can be expected to cause many foreign students to seek an American education. Soaring demand for first-rate education is a bright spot in the future of the research university. Research universities are likely to respond to robust demand in two ways: by continuing to raise tuition (especially the best public universities) and by placing more emphasis on teaching.

The key to this forecast is the continued growth of the college earnings premium. If the premium continues to rise, the tuition controversy is not likely to abate, but neither is the growing demand for a college education. Whether the earnings premium will decline depends on why it grew after 1980. One possibility is that it was caused by a deterioration in elementary and secondary schooling. If the earnings of those who do not attend college were depressed by poor precollege instruction, the trend in the earnings premium could be reversed by reforms in K-12 education that improve the qualifications and productivity of high school graduates. A much more likely explanation is that the college premium grew because of a shift in the demand for labor toward workers with the kinds of skills taught in college. If this shift in demand in favor of highly trained workers continues, the demand for higher education will persist. Researchers have so far been unable to identify the cause of the change in the earnings premium. Until they do, research universities will be uncertain whether the surging demand for a college diploma can last.

Endnotes

1. Lawrence E. Gladieux and Arthur M. Hauptman, *The College Aid Quandary: Access, Quality, and the Federal Role* (Brookings, 1995), p. 33.

2. Gladieux and Hauptman, *The College Aid Quandary*, p. 37. The sticker price of college includes tuition, room, board, books, and so on. It *excludes* the earnings that students give up while they are attending college (see below).

3. Ibid., p. 37.

4. Ibid., p. 37.

5. Data in this paragraph are from National Science Foundation, *Human Resources for Science and Technology: The European Region*, NSF Doc. 96–316 (Arlington, Va., 1996), pp. 85, 93, 97.

6. The classic work on this theme is Gary S. Becker, *Human Capital: A Theoretical and Empirical Analysis with Special Reference to Education* (Columbia University Press, 1975).

7. This figure is average cost minus average financial aid. Most likely, this is an overestimate, for financial aid is greater in more expensive institutions. The calculated returns to education are thus probably higher than the estimate in this paragraph.

8. Again, this is an overestimate of her lost earnings. The calculation assumes that she forgoes the average wage of high school graduates, whereas her earnings sacrifice is likely to be considerably less than this amount.

9. John Tsapogas, "Recent Engineering Graduates Out-Earn Their Science Counterparts," *National Science Foundation Data Brief*, November 8, 1996.

10. Jere R. Behrman, Mark R. Rosenzweig, and Paul Taubman, "College Choice and Wages: Estimates Using Data on Female Twins," *Review of Economics and Statistics*, vol. 76, no. 4 (November 1996), p. 674. In fact, Zvi Griliches and William Mason find that statistically controlling for the influence of individual ability tends to *increase* the estimated gain from attending college. Zvi Griliches and William M. Mason, "Education, Income, and Ability," *Journal of Political Economy*, vol. 80 (May/June, part 2, 1972), pp. S74–S103.

11. Larry L. Leslie and Paul T. Brinkman, *The Economic Value of Higher Education* (Macmillan, 1988).

12. See chapter 1 of this book.

13. Lewis Solmon, "The Definition and Impact of College Quality," in Lewis Solmon and Paul Taubman, *Does College Matter? Some Evidence on the Impacts of Higher Education* (Academic Press, 1973); Paul Taubman, *Sources of Inequality of Earnings* (Amsterdam: North-Holland, 1975); Paul Wachtel, "The Effects on Earnings of School and College Investment Expenditures," *Review of Economics and Statistics*, vol. 58 (1976), pp. 326–31; Terrence J. Wales, "The Effect of College Quality on Earnings: Results from the NBER-TH Data," *Journal of Human Resources*, vol. 7 (1973), pp. 306–317; Burton. A. Weisbrod and P. Karpoff, "Monetary Returns to College Education," *Review of Economics and Statistics*, vol. 50 (1968), pp. 491–97; and Behrman, Rosenzweig, and Taubman, "College Choice and Wages."

14. Behrman, Rosenzweig, and Taubman, "College Choice and Wages," pp. 672–85.

15. Ibid., p. 682.

16. Michael S. McPherson and Morton Owen Schapiro, "The Effect of Government Financing on the Behavior of Colleges and Universities," in Michael S. McPherson, Morton Owen Schapiro, and Gordon C. Winston, *Paying the Piper: Productivity, Incentives, and Financing Higher Education* (University of Michigan Press, 1993).

17. National Science Foundation, *Foreign Participation in U.S. Academic Science and Engineering: 1991*, NSF 93–302 (Washington, D.C., 1993), p. 39.

18. Ibid., pp. 9–10.

19. Ibid., pp. 11, 40.

20. National Science Foundation, *Science and Engineering Degrees, by Race/Ethnicity of Recipients, 1985–93*, NSF 95–330 (Arlington, Va., 1995), pp. 46, 48, 58, 60, 70, 72.

21. NSF, Foreign Participation, p. 40. Although the number of graduate degrees earned by foreigners continued to increase through 1995, foreign graduate enrollments in science and engineering fell by three percent between 1993 and 1994. (Dottie Jacobs, "Graduate Enrollments in Science and Engineering Decreased by 1 Percent in 1994," *National Science Foundation Data Brief.* July 24, 1996.) Because of the importance of science and engineering enrollments among foreign students, it is likely that total enrollments of foreigners in all fields also fell. The available data strongly suggest that the number of degrees earned by foreigners will soon begin to shrink. One should not interpret these data as signaling a relative decline in the quality of U.S. education, for the Chinese Student Protection Act of 1992 caused a surge of enrollments of Chinese students, as explained further in the main text.

22. National Science Foundation, *Undergraduate Origins of Recent (1991–95) Science and Engineering Doctorate Recipients*, NSF 96–334 (Arlington, Va., 1996), p. 23.

23. National Science Foundation, *Immigrant Scientists, Engineers, and Technicians 1991–92*, NSF 95–310 (Arlington, Va., 1995), p. 2.

24. National Science Foundation, *Immigrant Scientists, Engineers, and Technicians 1993*, NSF 9-322 (Arlington, Va., 1996), p. 7.

25. National Science Foundation, *Selected Data on Science and Engineering Doctorate Awards 1995*, NSF 96–303 (Arlington, Va., 1996), pp. 80–81.

26. National Science Foundation, *Characteristics of Doctoral Scientists and Engineers in the United States: 1993*, NSF 96–302 (Arlington, Va., 1996), p. 49.

27. William F. Massey and Charles A. Goldman, "The Production and Utilization of Science and Engineering Doctorates in the United States," August 1995.

28. National Science Foundation, *Characteristics of Doctoral Scientists and Engineers*, p. 17.

Chapter 4

The Outlook for Federal Support of University Research

Albert H. Teich

Six years ago, Leon Lederman, the president-elect of the American Association for the Advancement of Science (AAAS) released a report to the AAAS Board of Directors warning of a crisis in academic research. In the report *Science: The End of the Frontier?*, Lederman drew upon responses to an informal survey of nearly 250 scientists at U.S. universities to characterize the state of morale in academia, describing, in his words, "a depth of despair and discouragement that I have not experienced in my forty years in science. . . . The traditional optimism of research scientists," said Lederman, "is being quenched. In its place are lowered expectations and a gloomy vision of the future."[1]

The reason for the scientists' despair, according to the report, was no mystery. It was a lack of funding. Citing the enormous contributions that academic research has made to the U.S. economy, national security, health, and quality of life, Lederman called on the federal government to double its funding level

The views and opinions expressed in this chapter are those of the author writing as an individual and should not be taken to represent the positions of the American Association for the Advancement of Science, its Board, or its Council. This chapter was written in June 1996 and reflects the budget situation at that time.

(which in 1991 was about $10 billion a year) within the next two to three years.

The report received a great deal of attention. Members of the scientific community focused on the survey results and praised Lederman for bringing their plight to the public in a fair and realistic manner. The reaction in Washington, however, and especially on Capitol Hill, ranged from mild bemusement at the continuing naiveté of scientists to outrage at Lederman's failure to acknowledge that funding for science is not an entitlement.

Times have changed—and not for the better. Most academic scientists would probably look back at the federal funding situation and outlook as it was in 1991 with mild nostalgia for an era that seems to have ended. Today, the notion of doubling federal support for academic research in the near future seems well beyond our imagination. Just holding steady through the next decade would probably be regarded as a major victory by most university researchers and their Washington advocates. This shift has relatively little to do with public attitudes toward science, with such issues as "strategic" versus "curiosity-driven" research, or with any measurable change in the wishes of policymakers to capture the ongoing benefits research may bestow on society. It is best understood in the context of macropolitics and macrobudgeting, in which support for academic research is largely a residual issue.

U.S. Research and Development in Perspective

Notwithstanding the gloomy outlook for academic research, overall R&D in the United States remains a substantial enterprise. Funds from all sources expended on R&D in the United States during 1995 are estimated at about $171 billion.[2] In absolute terms, this is more than the combined expenditures of Japan, Germany, the United Kingdom, and France.[3] As a percentage of gross domestic product (GDP), however, U.S. R&D expenditures (at 2.4 percent) are less impressive, placing the United States somewhere in the middle among industrialized nations—above the United Kingdom and Italy, but below Japan and about equal to France and Germany.[4] Much of the U.S. investment is on the military side, where it has relatively little impact on the civilian economy. If we compare the ratio of nondefense R&D to GDP, the United States, at 1.9 percent, lags considerably behind Japan (2.7 percent) and Germany (2.4 percent).[5]

Nearly 60 percent of total R&D in the United States is supported by industrial firms with their own company funds. Most of the balance (35 percent) is supported by the federal government. Industry performs 70 percent of the nation's total R&D (supported both with firms' own funds and under federal contracts and grants), whereas academic institutions perform about 13 percent (a total of $21.6 billion, according to National Science Foundation statistics).[6]

About 60 percent of R&D in colleges and universities is supported by the federal government—about $13 billion in 1995. Among federal agencies, the largest supporter of university R&D is the National Institutes of Health (NIH), which provides more than 50 percent of the total. Other major supporters include the National Science Foundation (NSF, about 15 percent), the Department of Defense (DOD, about 12 percent), the National Aeronautics and Space Administration (NASA, 6 percent), and the Departments of Energy (DOE, 5 percent) and Agriculture (USDA, 3.5 percent). All of the remaining federal agencies—including, for example—the Departments of Commerce and Education and the Environmental Protection Agency (EPA) together provide only about 5 percent.[7]

The proportion of academic R&D supported by the federal government declined significantly between 1970 and 1992—dropping from 70.5 to 59.0 percent—as nonfederal sources, especially institutions' own funds and industry funds, grew more rapidly. However, during the past several years the trend has shifted, and the federal share has actually increased slightly since 1992. Over the past twenty-five years, industrial support of R&D in colleges and universities has grown from 2.6 percent of total academic R&D in 1970 to 6.9 percent in 1995. The share of institutional funds (which include general purpose state and local government appropriations, general purpose grants from nonfederal sources, tuition and fees, endowment income, unrestricted gifts, and licensing income) has grown from 10.4 to 18.1 percent over the same period.[8] Tables 4-1 and 4-2 present data on support of academic R&D by sector, for fiscal years 1975 through 1995, in current and constant dollars, respectively.

R&D in the Federal Budget

Federal R&D expenditures represent about 4.4 percent of the overall proposed federal budget for fiscal year 1997 and about 13.2 percent of the discretionary portion of that budget.[9] In the United States (in contrast with some nations) there is no overall budget for R&D and no special treatment of R&D in the budget. R&D programs are contained within the budgets of various federal agencies, in some cases (like NIH) representing a major share of the agency's budget and activities, in others (like the Department of Education or AID) a relatively small portion of a larger set of programs. Funding academic research is a primary mission at NSF and NIH and an important part of the overall research efforts in several other agencies.

Although the National Science and Technology Council (an interagency body chaired by the president and staffed by the White House Office of Science and Technology Policy) and the Office of Management and Budget (OMB) provide some coordination among the various agency R&D programs, the federal R&D effort is largely the sum of the individual agency programs. Coordination and priority-setting in R&D is made more difficult by the nature of the congressional budget process, which divides the federal budget among thirteen separate appropriations bills. R&D programs are included in ten of these bills; within these bills, most of these programs compete for budgetary priority mainly with other non-R&D programs, rather than with other R&D programs. Because of this, trade-offs are seldom made directly among R&D programs. They are made instead first among the missions of the agencies that contain these R&D programs, and then within those agencies (or others in the same appropriation bill) between R&D programs and other agency activities.

Table 4-1. *Support for Academic R&D, by Sector, Fiscal Years 1975–95, in Current Dollars*
Millions

Fiscal year	Total	Federal	State/ local	Industry	Academic institutions	All other
1975	3,409	2,288	332	113	417	259
1976	3,729	2,512	364	123	446	285
1977	4,067	2,726	374	139	514	314
1978	4,625	3,059	414	170	623	359
1979	5,366	3,598	472	193	735	368
1980	6,063	4,098	491	236	835	403
1981	6,847	4,571	546	292	1,004	435
1982	7,323	4,768	616	337	1,111	491
1983	7,881	4,989	626	389	1,302	576
1984	8,620	5,430	690	475	1,411	614
1985	9,686	6,063	752	560	1,617	694
1986	10,927	6,710	915	700	1,869	733
1987	12,152	7,342	1,023	790	2,169	828
1988	13,462	8,191	1,106	872	2,356	936
1989	14,975	8,988	1,223	995	2,698	1,071
1990	16,283	9,634	1,324	1,128	3,006	1,192
1991	17,577	10,230	1,473	1,205	3,362	1,307
1992	18,794	11,090	1,491	1,291	3,527	1,395
1993	19,911	11,957	1,559	1,374	3,552	1,469
1994[a]	20,950	12,600	1,600	1,450	3,750	1,550
1995[a]	21,600	13,000	1,600	1,500	3,900	1,600

Source: National Science Board, *Science & Engineering Indicators—1996*, NSB 96-21 (Government Printing Office, 1996), appendix table 5-2.
[a]1994 and 1995 figures are estimates.

The presumed disadvantage of this system is that there is no clear-cut way for the nation to assign an overall priority to federal support for R&D (or for academic research) and no easy means of setting priorities among different R&D fields. From the standpoint of the research community, the advantages include a diversity of sources of federal support and a net result that reflects not just the importance of R&D for its own sake, but the priority of the missions that R&D serves. As is the case for R&D as a whole, total federal support for R&D in colleges and universities is an after-the-fact sum of individual agency programs and decisions rather than a coordinated whole.

Table 4-2. *Support for Academic R&D, by Sector, Fiscal Years 1975–95, in Constant 1987 Dollars*

Millions

Fiscal year	Total	Federal	State/ local	Industry	Academic institutions	All other
1975	7,162	4,807	697	237	876	544
1976	7,283	4,906	711	240	871	557
1977	7,341	4,921	675	251	928	567
1978	7,760	5,133	695	285	1,045	602
1979	8,294	5,561	730	298	1,136	569
1980	8,588	5,805	695	334	1,183	571
1981	8,801	5,875	702	375	1,290	559
1982	8,760	5,703	737	403	1,329	587
1983	9,059	5,734	720	447	1,497	662
1984	9,483	5,974	759	523	1,552	675
1985	10,271	6,429	797	594	1,715	736
1986	11,253	6,910	942	721	1,925	755
1987	12,152	7,342	1,023	790	2,169	828
1988	12,994	7,906	1,068	842	2,274	903
1989	13,840	8,307	1,130	920	2,494	990
1990	14,538	8,602	1,182	1,007	2,684	1,064
1991	15,062	8,766	1,262	1,033	2,881	1,120
1992	15,649	9,234	1,241	1,075	2,937	1,162
1993	16,188	9,721	1,267	1,117	2,888	1,194
1994[a]	16,707	10,048	1,276	1,156	2,990	1,236
1995[a]	16,770	10,093	1,242	1,165	3,028	1,242

Source: National Science Board, *Science & Engineering Indicators—1996* (appendix table 5-2).
[a]1994 and 1995 figures are estimates.

Current Status of R&D in the Federal Budget

President Clinton's proposed budget for fiscal year 1997, released in March 1996, included $72.7 billion for R&D programs, an increase of 2.1 percent in current dollars, which translates into a more or less level budget in constant, inflation-adjusted terms. Within this total, nondefense R&D would increase by 5.2 percent, while defense R&D would decline 0.6 percent (in current dollars). The president's budget included an estimated $14.7 billion for basic research, an increase of slightly less than 2 percent. R&D in colleges and universities, which is largely but not entirely contiguous with basic research, is estimated at $12.7 billion in the president's budget, a 1.2 percent increase over fiscal year 1996. The distributions by agency of estimated federal support of basic research and R&D at colleges and universities for fiscal years 1995 through 1997 are shown in tables 4-3 and 4-4.[10]

The administration's spending proposals came on the heels of the fiscal year 1996 budget process that was the most protracted and contentious in recent memory. It was finally completed in late April 1996, nearly seven months into the fiscal year for which it was supposed to provide funds and almost fifteen months after the release of the president's fiscal year 1996 budget request. As the AAAS report on *Congressional Action on R&D in the FY 1996 Budget* relates, "In those fifteen months, the FY 1997 budget was submitted, the government shut down twice [once for over three weeks], a Republican Congress and a Democratic President fought over the proper size and role of the federal government, nearly a dozen different plans to balance the federal budget were considered, and many agencies operated from day to day under a record 13 temporary appropriations bills."[11]

On the whole, R&D programs fared better than many observers had expected in the early stages of the fiscal year 1996 budget process. The new Republican majority in Congress, led by an unusually zealous, conservative freshman class in the House, took office in January 1995 eager to implement its agenda, which had been laid out in the "Contract with America." This agenda called for sharp reductions in the size and scope of the federal government and for passage of a balanced budget amendment to the U.S. Constitution. When the amendment failed by one vote in the Senate, the leadership decided to use the existing budget process to accomplish its goals. These included eliminating the federal deficit by the year 2002, mainly through reductions in discretionary spending.

The budget battle began with two rescissions measures, taking back fiscal year 1995 funds that had been appropriated by the previous Congress. Defense R&D and nondefense R&D programs each lost about $1 billion in this process, not only cutting programs that were already in operation, but leaving a reduced base against which to measure fiscal year 1996 appropriations.

Table 4-3. *Estimated Federal Support for Basic Research by Agency,*
Fiscal Years 1995–97

Millions of dollars

	Fiscal year			Percent change, FY 1996–97	
Budget authority	1995 actual	1996 estimate	1997 budget	Current dollars	Constant dollars
Health and Human Services	6,068	6,441	6,557	1.8	–0.4
National Science Foundation	1,937	2,004	2,090	4.3	2.0
Defense	1,176	1,147	1,156	0.8	–1.4
Energy	1,621	1,960	2,035	3.8	1.6
National Aeronautics and Space Administration	1,968	1,890	1,826	–3.4	–5.5
Agriculture	600	590	615	4.2	2.0
Commerce	35	37	38	4.5	2.3
Interior	79	72	57	–20.2	–21.9
Transportation	36	39	45	15.4	12.9
Smithsonian Institute	131	132	144	9.1	6.7
Environmental Protection Agency	70	69	80	16.7	14.2
Veterans Affairs	16	17	17	0.0	–2.2
Education	8	6	8	33.3	30.5
Agency for International Development	0	1	0	–100.0	–100.0
Other	29	26	30	15.4	12.9
Total	13,772	14,430	14,699	1.9	—
Constant FY87 $	10,694	10,985	10,949	—	–0.3

Source: Intersociety Working Group, *AAAS Report XXI: Research and Development FY 1997*
(Washington: American Association for the Advancement of Science, 1996), table I-8.

Next, the congressional budget resolution, which received
final passage in June 1995, marked most nondefense discretionary
programs for sharp cuts in fiscal year 1996, followed by progres-
sive reductions in subsequent years through fiscal year 2002.
Most R&D programs (with a couple of significant exceptions)
were not targeted for cuts greater than the norm. In fact, the key
basic research agencies, NIH and NSF, were given somewhat
more favorable treatment. Nonetheless, when the effects of antic-

Table 4-4. *Estimated Federal Support for Conduct of R&D at Colleges and Universities by Agency, Fiscal Years 1995–97*
Millions of dollars

	Fiscal year			Percent change, FY 1996–97	
Budget authority	1995 actual	1996 estimate	1997 budget	Current dollars	Constant dollars
Health and Human Services	6,654	6,995	7,117	1.7	–0.3
National Science Foundation	1,964	1,957	1,980	1.2	–0.6
Defense	1,541	1,458	1,413	–3.1	–3.0
National Aeronautics and Space Administration	815	792	813	2.7	0.3
Energy	627	599	573	–4.3	–3.7
Agriculture	428	414	411	–0.7	–1.7
Interior	50	51	42	–18.3	–11.6
Transportation	53	59	68	15.3	7.4
Environmental Protection Agency	130	107	130	21.5	10.9
Commerce	69	64	58	–9.4	–6.6
Education	101	66	109	65.2	35.7
Veterans Administration	2	2	0	–100.0	–58.0
Nuclear Regulatory Commission	6	2	3	50.0	27.1
U.S. Postal Service	3	4	4	0.0	–1.2
Labor	1	1	1	0.0	–1.2
Social Security Administration	1	2	2	0.0	–1.2
Total	12,445	12,573	12,724	1.2	—
Constant FY87 $	9,663	9,571	9,477	—	–1.0

Source: Intersociety Working Group, *AAAS Report XXI: Research and Development, FY 1997* (Washington: American Association for the Advancement of Science, 1996), table I-9.

ipated inflation were taken into account, the net result was the projection of a one-third reduction in real (inflation-adjusted) spending for nondefense R&D over the seven-year period.[12]

But political reality—in the form of public opinion, interest group lobbying, threatened and actual presidential vetoes, and internal splits within the Republican party—intervened between the budget resolution and the final appropriations for fiscal year 1996. The details of the budget resolution are not binding on appropriators; when the dust finally settled on appropriations, the reductions in many areas were far less than had been indicated earlier. NSF's R&D, which had been marked for an 8.8 percent cut in fiscal year 1996, received slightly more R&D funding ($4 million, or 0.2 percent) than it had in fiscal year 1995. A projected 11.4 percent cut in the budget resolution for R&D at NASA turned into a 0.5 percent reduction in appropriations. DOE, threatened with a 21.5 percent cut in its nondefense R&D, wound up losing 9.0 percent. NIH ultimately ended up with a nearly $700 million increase (6.3 percent) in place of the 2.1 percent reduction that had been called for by the budget resolution. Overall, nondefense R&D in fiscal year 1996 was down slightly more than 1 percent relative to fiscal year 1995—unimpressive ordinarily, but a considerable improvement over the budget resolution's projected 12.4 percent reduction. Total basic research, led by the appropriations increase at NIH, was up nearly 5 percent.[13]

As a result of this turn of events, the impact of the fiscal year 1996 budget on academic research was less damaging than anticipated. NIH's modest real-dollar increase (above the rate of inflation) provided a modicum of growth for biomedical science in universities and medical schools. NSF's research directorates, which did a bit better than the agency as a whole, also had slightly more to spend in fiscal year 1996 than in fiscal year 1995—although, according to recent figures, most of the growth did not seem likely to redound to the benefit of universities and colleges. The four other federal agencies that make up the remainder of the "big six" supporters of academic research—DOD, NASA, DOE, and USDA—all projected R&D funding declines of 3 to 5 percent in current dollars, suggesting a tight year in those departments and research centers (mainly in the physical sciences, engineering, and agriculture) which draw significant amounts of support from these sponsors.

Fiscal Year 1997 and the Years Ahead

On the whole, the president's R&D proposals for fiscal year 1997 did not differ markedly from his plans for prior years. Modest reductions in defense R&D and increases in nondefense R&D helped bring the ratio of defense to nondefense R&D closer to the 50/50 goal announced early in the Clinton administration. Programs aimed at building partnerships between the government and the private sector and encouraging the development of technologies to improve U.S. industrial competitiveness received special emphasis, as they had in prior years, despite Republican opposition to such programs and congressional efforts to eliminate them. The Clinton administration's support for environmental research programs, some of which were also targeted for sharp reductions by Congress in 1995, was reaffirmed in the proposed budget.

Congressional attitudes toward the Clinton proposals, as was already evident from the early stages of the congressional budget process, paralleled those of 1995. Nevertheless, the Republican congressional leadership was aware that its confrontational strategy backfired then, ultimately strengthening the president's hand and tilting public opinion in his favor. That, combined with the compressed time frame resulting from the 1996 party conventions and the fall election, produced an atmosphere more conducive to compromise than would otherwise be the case. The outcome for R&D programs was similar to the fiscal year 1996 outcome, minus the brinksmanship, shutdowns, and inflammatory rhetoric: a flat or slightly increased budget for NSF; a more significant increase for NIH; small reductions for DOE, NASA, DOD science and technology, and USDA; and somewhat larger reductions for the smaller R&D agencies.

If this suggests another year of muddling through, it is perhaps as much as can be expected from a governmental system torn by divisions as deep and goals as conflicting as those evident in the United States today. However, this leaves unresolved the course of research in coming years—the so-called out-years in which both Congress and the president have vowed to bring the budget into balance. These out-years are a source of major concern to the research community.

As noted earlier, the fiscal year 1996 congressional budget resolution projected a seven-year decline in discretionary spending, resulting in an inflation-adjusted one-third cut in nondefense

R&D by fiscal year 2002. The president's original out-year projections in the fiscal year 1996 budget did not contain enough detail to permit direct comparison with this number, but his out-year numbers for the total budgets of several R&D-intensive agencies (including NASA, DOE, and NSF) suggested substantial future reductions for R&D. (Administration spokespersons, however, did stress repeatedly that these out-year numbers were not definitive and that the president, recognizing research as an investment in the future, intended to shelter it from major reductions.)

The out-year picture in the fiscal year 1997 budget was not materially different from that of fiscal year 1996. The fiscal year 1997 administration budget does contain detailed out-year projections as part of its plan to balance the budget by fiscal year 2002. As originally presented in March 1996, these projections show declines in most discretionary program budgets (including R&D programs) beginning in fiscal year 1998, after fiscal year 1997's increases. The budgets bottom out in fiscal year 2000. At that point nondefense R&D would be down about 19 percent in constant dollars from its original fiscal year 1995 level, then increase in fiscal year 2001, recovering to about 12 percent below fiscal year 1995 by fiscal year 2002.[14]

The upturn was based on OMB's relatively optimistic forecast of economic conditions at the millennium. However, in the course of the fiscal year 1996 bargaining, the president had agreed to base his balanced budget plan on the Congressional Budget Office (CBO) economic forecasts (which are also used by Congress). Therefore, the president's March 1996 budget contained a footnote indicating that the fiscal year 2001 and 2002 projections were contingent on CBO's certifying that his proposed budget does indeed balance. If not, the footnote stated, the reductions needed to bring the budget into balance would be taken entirely from the discretionary portion of the budget.

CBO's report, issued in mid-April 1996, indicated that it would be necessary to make substantial reductions in discretionary spending in the last two years of the period to bring the president's budget into balance. Although the administration did not issue new projections, AAAS calculated the impact of the cuts required by CBO's estimates on R&D, applying the reductions evenly across the board in discretionary programs. In these adjusted projections, overall nondefense R&D would be down by about 25 percent in constant dollars by fiscal year 2002.

The story was much the same in the fiscal year 1997 congressional budget resolution. AAAS's analysis indicates that under its assumptions, total nondefense R&D was projected to decline 23.0 percent between fiscal year 1995 and fiscal year 2002, in inflation-adjusted terms. The fact that the presidential and congressional budgets both arrive at more or less the same point by fiscal year 2002 is perhaps less surprising than it may seem. After all, they not only share the same economic assumptions (those of CBO), but they also both place the heaviest burden of deficit reduction on discretionary spending, the category that includes R&D. In fact, were it not for a reduction in the forecast rate of inflation (2.0 to 2.2 percent a year through the end of the period in the current forecast, compared with 3.0 to 3.5 percent a year in the fiscal year 1996 forecast), the cut in R&D in both the administration and congressional budgets would be quite close to the fiscal year 1996 congressional budget projection of a one-third cut. Table 4-5 displays a comparison of the out-year projections for nondefense R&D in the major civilian agencies in the president's fiscal year 1997 budget (as adjusted by AAAS) and in the congressional budget resolution.

There are major differences between the two plans:

—The president's budget requested an increase in R&D in fiscal year 1997, whereas the budget resolution projects a cut.

—Because of the differences in the slope of the two curves, the aggregate total that would be spent on R&D under the Clinton administration's plan between now and fiscal year 2002 would be greater than under the congressional plan.

—The relative priority given to various agencies is different in the two plans, with the president favoring the administration's technology initiatives within the Department of Commerce as well as some of its priorities in energy R&D in the Department of Energy, and NASA and NSF coming out somewhat better in the congressional plan.

Should a reduction along these lines actually take place, the impact on the U.S. research system and the universities that rep-

Table 4-5. *Projected Federal Spending on Nondefense R&D, Fiscal Year 1995–2002*
Millions of current U.S. dollars

	R&D FY 1995 original[a]	R&D FY 1996 est.	R&D FY 1997 est.	R&D FY 1998 est.	R&D FY 1999 est.	R&D FY 2000 est.	R&D FY 2001 est.	R&D FY 2002 est.	FY 2002 in constant 1995 U.S. $[b]	% change in constant U.S. $, 1995–2002
NIH (President)	10,840	11,443	11,901	11,901	11,901	11,901	11,337	10,788	9,273	-14.5
NIH (Congress)	10,840	11,443	11,446	11,446	11,446	11,446	11,446	11,445	9,838	-9.2
NASA (President)	9,875	9,416	9,700	8,908	8,443	7,972	8,073	8,185	7,036	-28.7
NASA (Congress)	9,875	9,416	9,316	8,946	8,845	8,772	8,769	8,897	7,648	-22.5
DOE nondefense (President)	3,969	3,577	3,866	3,798	3,314	3,141	3,187	3,237	2,782	-29.9
DOE nondefense (Congress)	3,969	3,577	3,456	2,899	2,782	2,688	2,631	2,507	2,224	-44.0
NSF (President)	2,544	2,401	2,479	2,485	2,491	2,497	2,379	2,264	1,946	-23.5
NSF (Congress)	2,544	2,401	2,464	2,460	2,498	2,566	2,647	2,758	2,371	-6.8%
USDA (President)	1,540	1,425	1,444	1,337	1,228	1,116	1,166	1,218	1,047	-32.0
USDA (Congress)	1,540	1,425	1,425	1,262	1,288	1,297	1,341	1,419	1,220	-20.8
All other R&D (President)	5,544	4,484	5,051	4,939	4,797	4,648	4,541	4,460	3,834	-30.8

	R&D FY 1995 original[a]	R&D FY 1996 est.	R&D FY 1997 est.	R&D FY 1998 est.	R&D FY 1999 est.	R&D FY 2000 est.	R&D FY 2001 est.	R&D FY 2002 est.	FY 2002 in constant 1995 U.S. $[b]	% change in constant U.S. $, 1995–2002
All other R&D (Congress)	5,544	4,484	4,063	4,678	3,648	3,610	3,613	3,615	3,107	–43.9
Total nondefense R&D										
President	34,312	32,746	34,441	33,368	32,174	31,275	30,683	30,152	25,918	–24.5
Congress	34,312	32,746	32,170	30,781	30,507	30,378	30,446	30,723	25,408	–23.0

Souce: Summary of two AAAS analyses. *Projected Effects of President's FY 1997 Budget Outyear Projections on Nondefense R&D—Adjusted for Spring 1996 CBO Forecast* (May 17, 1996); *Projected Effects on Concurrent (Final) FY 1997 Budget Resolution on Nondefense R&D* (corrected version; June 21, 1996). For agency and program details, and detailed information on methodology, please refer to these analyses.

[a]This analysis uses the original fiscal year 1995 funding level as the baseline to reflect the seven-year timetable for balancing the budget.

[b]Expressed in fiscal year dollars; adjusted for inflation according to GDP deflators. Fiscal year 1995 R&D figures are before rescissions enacted in 1995. Fiscal year 1996 figures represent the latest AAS estimate on R&D in fiscal year 1996 appropriations fiscal year 1997–2002 figures are AAAS estimates based on porjections contained in the president's fiscal year 1997 budget and the proposed House fiscal year 1997 budget resolution policy assumptions, adjusted for changes in the final budget resolution. The two analyses are available on the World Wide Web at http://www.aaas.org/spp/dspp/rd/rdwwwpg.htm

resent a key part of it would certainly be substantial. The system would survive, but there is no question that it would be radically changed. Rather than speculating on the nature of these changes or on the prospects for replacing federal funds with those from other sources (which seem remote), it would seem more useful at this point to consider the meaning of these out-year projections and the political context of the R&D elements within them.

Out-year projections, it should be stressed, are simply *projections*. They are something between plans and scenarios and are not carved in stone, nor even written into law. Nothing binds future congresses or administrations to follow these projections. In fact, past experience suggests that they have limited predictive value. Under the out-year projections contained in the Reagan and Bush administration budgets of the 1980s and early 1990s and the congressional budget resolutions of those eras, the federal budget would have been balanced years ago and the nation would today be running a comfortable surplus. On the other hand, in past years the out-year projections for most R&D agencies generally showed an upward trend—even under those earlier balanced budget scenarios. The trends in current projections are so uniformly negative that it is difficult to escape the expectation that there will be less federal money available for R&D programs in the future than there is today—although how much less is unclear.

What the out-year projections show are the policy choices and trade-offs the administration and Congress say they are willing to make to achieve a balanced budget. Both would do so primarily through cuts in discretionary spending, including cuts to most of the discretionary budget accounts funding R&D. They would also allow spending on mandatory programs such as social security, medicare, and medicaid to increase at a rate greater than inflation.

With only a couple of exceptions in areas of significant political controversy (mainly the administration's civilian technology development programs), the projected reductions in R&D are not the result of any antipathy political leaders of either party have toward science and technology, R&D, or universities. Indeed the broad-based bipartisan support for the nation's R&D (especially basic research) remains largely intact, despite the end of the cold war. Rather, the reductions in R&D programs are the fallout from efforts to balance the federal budget by reducing discretionary spending.

All of this suggests that the budget problems facing U.S. universities and the research system transcend the domain in which science policy is discussed and shaped. Over the past four decades (except in the 1960s, during the heyday of the Apollo space program), trends in nondefense R&D spending have closely followed trends in overall nondefense discretionary spending, while trends in total federal R&D (including defense) have tracked total discretionary spending. Despite the highly decentralized nature of R&D funding in the United States, R&D has consistently hovered near 14 percent of total discretionary spending. Seen in a broad national perspective, the expansion of federal investment in R&D over the past several decades has therefore resulted not only from a commitment to the "endless frontier" of science and technology, but also (and perhaps as importantly) from the general growth in discretionary spending that has provided an umbrella for growth in a wide range of government programs, including R&D. If, as President Clinton and others have said, "the era of big government is over," and if Congress and the president continue to pursue a balanced budget primarily through cuts in discretionary spending, especially nondefense discretionary funds, then further cuts to federal support of R&D and academic research are inevitable.[15]

Endnotes

1. Leon M. Lederman, *Science: The End of the Frontier?*, report from the president-elect to the AAAS Board of Directors (Washington: American Association for the Advancement of Science, January 1991), pp. 3, 6.

2. National Science Board, *Science & Engineering Indicators–1996*, NSB Doc. 96-21 (Government Printing Office, 1996), p. 4-4.

3. National Science Board, *Science & Engineering Indicators–1996*, p. 4-35.

4. Ibid., appendix table 4-33, p. 154.

5. National Science Board, *Science & Engineering Indicators–1996*, appendix table 4-34, p. 155.

6. Ibid., pp. 4-5, 4-6.

7. Ibid., appendix table 5-8, p. 177.

8. Ibid., pp. 5-7 to 5-9 and appendix table 5-2, p. 167.

9. Intersociety Working Group, *AAAS Report XXI: Research & Development, FY 1997* (Washington: American Association for the Advancement of Science, 1996), table I-2, p. 48.

10. Ibid., table I-5, p. 51, and table I-8, p. 54.

11. Kei Koizumi and others, *Congressional Action on R&D in the FY 1996 Budget* (Washington: American Association for the Advancement of Science, 1996), p. 5.

12. Albert H. Teich and others, *Interim Report on Congressional Appropriations for R&D in FY 1996* (Washington: American Association for the Advancement of Science, August 1995), p. 6.

13. Percentage changes derived from data posted on the AAAS R&D Budget & Policy Project World Wide Web site, http://www.aaas.org/spp/dspp/rd/rdwwwpg.htm, and contained in *Congressional Action on R&D in the FY 1996 Budget*.

14. Data from AAAS World Wide Web site, http://www.aaas.org/spp/dspp/rd/rdwwwpg.htm.

15. Portions of this paragraph have been adapted from Albert H. Teich, "An Introduction to R&D in the Federal Budget," in Intersociety Working Group, *AAAS Report XXI*, chapter 1, pp. 5–11.

Chapter 5

The Economics of University Indirect Cost Reimbursement in Federal Research Grants

Roger G. Noll and William P. Rogerson

The purpose of this chapter is to explore the nature and causes of the increasingly fractious relationship between universities and the federal government regarding the reimbursement of indirect costs, or overhead, in federally sponsored research, and to propose some new ways to think about and perhaps ameliorate this problem. On the basis of the analysis in this chapter, we have concluded that the source of this friction is the method that the federal government uses to pay for university research, not the intentions or integrity of either party. In particular, the methods that the government uses to pay for indirect costs distort the incentives of both universities and federal agencies and lead to wasteful expenditures by both. To solve this problem requires fundamentally changing the form of federal research grants to universities.

The federal government pays for university research grants through cost-based contracts similar to the procedures that are used to pay defense contractors for weapons system development.[1] The amount awarded is based on projected costs, and the university can keep only that portion of the award for which it can document that these costs were incurred. Federal research grants are therefore essentially contracts under which the university promises to undertake a project and to monitor the expenses incurred in doing so. The federal government agrees to pay the estimated cost of the project when work is initiated and to let the university keep the monies for appropriately documented expenses for the project. This method of funding is often called, inaccurately, "full cost reimbursement" because it is based on the idea that the government pays for all costs of research it supports.[2]

To support cost-based contracting (and to determine reimbursement), the federal government requires universities to establish elaborate government-approved and government-audited accounting systems for calculating the cost of research projects. The incentive for principal investigators and universities to perform high-quality research is generated by the process of competitive awards based on peer review. Simply put, the prospects of being awarded future grants and obtaining other benefits to one's professional reputation provide the incentives for performing high-quality research.

On average, approximately 70 percent of a federal research grant to a university consists of so-called direct costs: costs that can be easily and nonarbitrarily associated with performing a single research project. These include the salaries of personnel and the cost of lab equipment and supplies used in the project.[3] The other 30 percent of grant awards is for "indirect costs." In theory, indirect costs are joint costs of numerous university activities that cannot be attributed to any particular project. The largest components of overhead costs are administration and the depreciation, operation, and maintenance of buildings and equipment.[4]

Although indirect costs account for much less than half of the total cost of federal research grants, they are the source of a great deal of public controversy. The most visible controversies have centered on the issue of whether universities include inappropriate expenses in federal overhead costs, such as the president's expenses for entertaining university trustees or depreciation of the university yacht. More generally, overhead expenditures are widely regarded as too high, in part because the cost-based contracting system encourages universities to add unnecessary expenses to their overhead accounts. Of course, university indirect costs are not high compared with other kinds of federal R&D contracts. For example, in the aerospace industry, indirect costs accounted for 58 percent of total contract costs, roughly double the percentage at universities.[5] Nevertheless, the anecdotal improprieties have created a perception of inefficiency as well as pressures to undertake reforms.

Thus far, the main response to the indirect cost controversy has been for government and universities to devote more and more resources to calculating and auditing overhead costs. This process itself is a major cause of the increase in overhead expenses because administering the accounting system is itself treated as an overhead cost! More fundamentally, in times of declining federal budgets, some have questioned whether government ought to be paying any overhead expenses at all. The rationale for this position is that the government has no obligation to pay indirect costs; the university would have to incur most of these expenditures even if no federal research were performed.

We believe that the fundamental cause of controversies regarding indirect cost recovery is neither inadequate effort in implementing accounting and auditing systems nor mismanagement on the part of either universities or granting agencies. Instead, the fundamental problem is the very concept of using a system of retrospective cost reimbursement to calculate indirect cost rates. In particular, we propose that federal grants pay for university overhead cost through a prospective standards-based reimbursement system. In such a system, overhead rates for all universities are determined through periodic audits of a small sample of similar universities. In particular, a university's reimbursement for indirect costs would not depend on its own accounting estimates of its overhead costs. A prospective reimbursement system of this sort would sharpen the incentive to manage overhead costs efficiently, remove a number of other distortions created by the current cost-based system, and drastically lower the cost of accounting for and administering federal grants, while still providing adequate support for high-quality research.

Our proposal is similar in spirit to regulatory reforms currently sweeping through a wide variety of regulated industries and to the changes under way in paying for health services. The idea is that when many firms are producing similar products, reimbursement for any particular firm can be based on the average cost of all of the firms. This form of payment severs the link between a firm's costs and its reimbursement and creates incentives for individual firms to manage their costs efficiently. This idea motivated the prospective payment diagnostic related group (DRG) system for medicare payments to hospitals and has been applied by state and federal regulators in electricity, transportation, and telecommunications.

In the next section, we describe the contracting problem that the government faces in supporting university research. We then describe the general approach the government has taken to solve this problem through its cost-based reimbursement system. Finally, we explain why this system works so poorly when applied to overhead costs, and why prospective reimbursement would work much better.

The Nature of the R&D Contracting Problem

As discussed in chapter 2, a university can be viewed as a firm producing several outputs, including education and research. Neither of these outputs can be measured accurately. Educational output is measured by years of study, scores on tests, and numbers of various degrees awarded, but these measures do not adequately measure educational quality. Research is even more complex. New ideas cannot be measured or weighed. Furthermore, in addition to new ideas, an output of research is improved capabilities and competencies in the faculty and students who perform it. As a result, providing objectively verifiable measures of a university's educational output is difficult, and objectively measuring a university's research output is essentially impossible.

The key consequence of the difficulty in measuring output is that the federal government and universities cannot write research contracts based on measured output. This point is extremely significant. When the output of the activity can be adequately measured in some objectively verifiable fashion, the contracting problem is easy to solve. Firms offer proposals describing what they will produce and what they will charge; government then selects the offer that gives the best value. A simple competitive bidding process for a well-defined product creates no need for retrospective cost-based contracting.

The problem with R&D procurement is that the parties cannot base their contract on outputs. About the only aspect of a research program that can be measured objectively is the university's expenditures on inputs. Therefore, not surprisingly, R&D contracts are essentially contracts over inputs instead of outputs. That is, in a research contract, a university promises to make certain types of expenditures. The federal government then makes payments on the basis of cost estimates secured by an offer of proof that the university spent the funds in the way promised. The purpose of the accounting system required by the government is to provide objectively verifiable measures of these expenditures.

By contractually specifying what sorts of expenditures the university will make, the federal government gains a fair measure of control over the nature and type of research to be done. Clearly, a principal investigator cannot spend funds intended for performing experiments on a particle accelerator to study yak breeding in Nepal without running the risk of being detected. Therefore, contracting over inputs provides the government with some contractual control over the variable it is truly concerned about, which is the output of research. Consequently, cost-based reimbursement is a natural and logical approach to R&D contracting.

A weakness of a contract over expenditures is that it provides no direct incentive for a principal investigator or a university to conduct high-quality research. In the present system, the incentives for high-quality research operate primarily through the reputation-building effects of excellent work. To the individual investigator, a professional reputation is acquired by establishing priority in findings and thereby having one's name associated with new ideas; this, in turn, facilitates obtaining more financial support for research that will finance producing still more results and gaining an even greater reputation.[6] Similarly, high-quality research is useful to a university in attracting students, gifts from private donors, and more federal grants.

The importance of the reputational value of good research is enhanced by using competition and peer review to award federal grants. Among the factors affecting peer judgment are the principal investigator's performance on previous projects and the university's reputation for providing a supportive and productive research environment. This reputational mechanism neatly finesses the problem of objectively measuring research outputs. It may not be possible to base legally enforceable contracts for a particular project on expert evaluations regarding the worth of the research, but it is possible to base next period's award on these judgments.

For this reputational mechanism to provide a significant incentive for universities, the university must regard obtaining future grants as important. That is, some sort of prize must be attached to being awarded a research grant, and a larger prize will create a greater incentive to provide an environment that nurtures and supports high-quality research.

Overhead Costs in Contractual Relationships

Approximately 30 percent of the costs incurred by universities are indirect or overhead costs, and most indirect costs are for central administration and the depreciation, operation, and maintenance of buildings and equipment. The distinction between indirect and direct costs is closely related to the concept of incremental or marginal cost, which is the additional cost of undertaking an activity, given that all of the other activities of the organization will still be undertaken.

Overhead costs have two defining characteristics: invariance and opacity. For the most part, indirect costs are not incremental or marginal with respect to any single activity of the university. That is, if a particular research project were canceled, total overhead expenditures would be almost completely unaffected. Indeed, even if the university scaled back its research efforts substantially, it would still need to incur a large part of its overhead to operate its educational activities. Similarly, if the university scaled back its education efforts, much of the overhead cost would still be needed to support its research activities.

Even if an indirect cost element is partially incremental with respect to a particular activity, the precise extent to which it is incremental is almost impossible to measure in a way that any accounting system could implement. Accounting systems cannot conduct the thought experiment of estimating the long-term effect of a change in university activities on overhead costs.

A persistent issue in federal research policy is whether and to what extent university research grants ought to pay for overhead expenditures. To the extent that indirect costs are not incremental for any particular activity, the university would still incur them to accomplish its remaining activities, even if the federal government supported no research at the university. However, if these costs are not paid by someone, the university will be unable to accomplish anything because it will become financially unviable. The fact that indirect costs are not incremental does not make them any less real or make paying them any less necessary to the university's survival as an institution.

A second issue pertaining to indirect cost recovery concerns monitoring and reviewing these costs to determine if they are "reasonable." For direct costs this function is largely performed through reviewing proposals. In a proposal, the principal investigator lists in some detail the direct costs to be incurred by a research project. Before the proposal is submitted, university administrators check these costs to ensure that specific cost items (including indirect costs) are accurate. They also determine that the proposal does not commit the university to perform a project that will cost far more than the amount requested. After the proposal is submitted, the awarding agency makes a broad assessment as to whether the proposed costs seem appropriate and necessary. Because indirect costs are not directly associated with any particular research project, the granting agency cannot make such a determination with respect to overhead costs. We argue later in this chapter that the best policy response to this problem is to create incentives for universities to manage overhead costs themselves. This is a better choice than devoting substantial resources to measuring whether the costs incurred are necessary and reasonable.

Government and University Objectives

To design an effective contracting mechanism between universities and the federal agencies that support research, one must first understand each party's objectives in contracting for research. In this case, precisely specifying the goals of both parties is quite difficult. Both government agencies and universities are nonprofit institutions; as a result, their objectives cannot be reduced to simple measures of financial performance, as is the case for businesses. Whereas the goals of nonprofit institutions are not thoroughly understood, the discussion in chapter 2 suggests some plausible motivations: growing as large as possible; accomplishing certain social goals that managers view as desirable; and maximizing managerial status, recognition, perquisites, and benefits. Because universities are managed in large measure by senior faculty, the latter goals can be interpreted as serving social objectives widely shared among faculty members and maximizing the status and welfare of faculty.

To obtain the funds necessary to achieve these objectives, both agencies and universities must satisfy certain external constituencies. Consequently, to attain their core objectives, nonprofit organizations must be oriented to serve these groups. Because both government agencies and universities must respond to numerous constituencies, they pursue complex, multidimensional objectives that partially (but not completely) overlap. Differences in objectives are at the heart of the controversies over federal grants to universities. These differences create the contracting problem that must be overcome to make federally sponsored university research as efficient as possible.

Federal grant programs for sponsoring university research presumably serve three purposes:

—To achieve the specific research objectives that are promised in a successful proposal;

—To accomplish more general objectives concerning the strength and topical breadth of the nation's research capabilities; and

—To strengthen the educational system for students in technical disciplines.

Whereas these objectives are to some extent complementary, they are also distinct enough to require separate attention if each is to be attained efficiently.

For the purposes of this chapter, the main implication of the multiplicity of government goals is that the federal government arguably has a fairly large interest in supporting university indirect costs. Overhead supports other activities in addition to federally sponsored research projects that the government values. More generally, the federal government must explicitly identify and design mechanisms within the grant system to assure that the broader purposes of support for research universities are taken into account.

An important feature of the implementation of federal R&D policy through numerous sponsoring agencies is that in an agency that supports university research, a balance among government's objectives is unlikely to arise. Each agency will be held accountable for achieving the narrow goals embodied in its project grants. Yet each agency will bear less of a responsibility for the overall health of U.S. academic research and education, because the latter objectives derive support from many agencies and other sources. Consequently, proactive participation in overall academic research policy by the centralized agencies in the Executive Office of the President—like the Office of Management and Budget (OMB) or the one diverse source of academic research support, the National Science Foundation (NSF)—is necessary to balance the more narrow focus that is likely to predominate in the more specialized, focused agencies. Placing responsibility for making indirect cost recovery policy in more focused agencies, such as the Department of Defense, is likely to lead to less generous reimbursement and a weaker university system than would result if this responsibility were given to NSF.

For research universities, attaining the objectives of growth and prestige requires obtaining support from numerous constituencies other than the federal government: students and their families, private donors (including industry), state and local government, and consumers of other university services such as health care and sporting events. Universities also are largely democratic, with faculty playing an important role in university governance.

Two qualitative properties of the preferences of research universities can be deduced from these observations.

First, and perhaps most important, because grants are a major source of funds for research universities, federal research policy has an enormous effect on what universities do. Universities do not naturally and altruistically strive for research excellence independently of federal grants. In fact, most universities in the United States, and nearly all universities worldwide, do not support extensive research. Federal spending on high-quality research in science and engineering allows some universities to grow and to prosper by becoming strong in these areas. However, there is no reason to believe that universities are inherently more predisposed to foster high-quality technical research than to produce high-quality football teams.

In addition, to the extent that pressures brought on by students, private donors, and faculty influence universities to value research, universities are likely to prefer more diversity in study areas and balance across fields than the federal government displays in grant policies. Universities and the federal government have overlapping goals only with respect to the health of research in areas that the government supports, but even in these areas there are two main sources of conflict. Each university seeks to maximize its own standing as a research institution. (Harvard is unlikely to make sacrifices to assure that Princeton remains strong.) In addition, universities are willing to sacrifice some strength in a strong field that receives federal support to improve quality in a weak field that lacks such support but that other university constituencies value.

The main conclusion that follows from this discussion of goals is simply that universities and the federal government do not share the same objectives. In particular, the correct way to view the federal government's problem is that it is truly an incentive-contracting problem. The government must seek to design institutions and contracts that create incentives for universities to act more in the way the government prefers, and less in the way that universities would prefer if federal money came with no strings attached.

In ordinary market transactions with for-profit firms, the federal government creates incentives by allowing firms to earn a profit if the results sought are achieved. The fact that defense contractors must earn a profit is a reality that must be taken into account in designing the defense contracting system.[7] Analogously, in transactions with universities the federal government must permit something like profits on activities that it wants to encourage, knowing full well that the university will then use these funds to pay for activities the federal government does not value so highly. This analog to profits provides the university with the incentive to undertake activities that the government prefers. Therefore, for incentive-based reasons, the government usually will find it worthwhile to pay more than cost. Economic actors that are always paid at cost and nothing more have no incentive to spend efficiently or to produce results that the sponsor wants.

The second conclusion that follows from these observations is that the net cost to the federal government of allowing universities to earn a profit on sponsored research is much lower than the gross amount of the profit, for three reasons. Some of the profit will be used to support activities the federal government values but does not support directly. In addition, the possibility for profit, if properly designed, will increase the university's incentive to undertake its work more efficiently than would be the case under a cost-reimbursement contract. Finally, the prospect of profit will give the entire university—not just the grant recipient—a stake in maintaining the quality of federally sponsored research, thereby increasing output per dollar of effort.

Alternatives to Contracting

Given the problems with contracting for R&D, the question that naturally arises is whether the federal government could better respond to these problems by avoiding contracting altogether and conducting more R&D in government research labs. Reflecting the problems of contracting for research, private companies typically undertake virtually all research in their own research divisions.[8] In other nations a far larger fraction of government-supported research is undertaken in government-operated laboratories, rather than through companies or universities. Indeed, in many countries both universities and industries that perform government-sponsored research are nationalized.

Undertaking work within the same organization facilitates controlling the quality and quantity of resources devoted to a project, monitoring the efforts of research personnel, and practicing flexible project management that changes the character of research activities as work proceeds and new information is acquired. In addition, internal systems of reward and punishment can be based on cumulative measures of career performance by researchers and research managers, rather than on the success or failure of any particular project, and tied to the long-term success of the organization.

Three rationales for the U.S. approach can be offered.

The origin of the U.S. system was probably in part purely political. Decentralization serves the ideological preference for less direct government control, as well as the political interests of members of Congress who want to spread federal spending over many states and districts.

In addition, the highly decentralized U.S. approach offers the compensation of diversity. Because the value of research is inherently uncertain, the most effective national research policy may be to attack numerous problems (and each significant problem in many ways) to take advantage of the specialized knowledge of different researchers in various institutional settings.[9] This strategy maximizes the chance that the most important research results will be found. Because fundamental research is inexpensive compared with most attempts to apply new knowledge on a commercial scale, a diverse set of initial projects may pay for itself by focusing more expensive subsequent activities on projects with the highest expected return. In the public sector, diversity cannot be attained if a central authority (ultimately, Congress and the president) directly manages all federally sponsored research.

Finally, even if research is centralized, many of the same incentive problems occur within the organization.[10] In a huge, centralized research organization, top managers face the difficult problem of measuring their researchers' productivity and providing them with sharp incentives to do the work most valuable to managers rather than projects most appealing to researchers.

For some combination of these reasons, the federal government supports a relatively decentralized R&D program through contracting with universities. For the purposes of this chapter, we simply take this decision as given. The relevant question then becomes how contracting methods might be improved.

The Mechanics of Cost-Based Reimbursement

Because of the inherent difficulties in writing performance contracts for R&D, the federal government has chosen to use cost-reimbursement according to a set of government-mandated accounting principles and negotiated accounting and auditing methods. Although the federal government has always used a system of cost reimbursement, based on accounting records, to pay the direct costs of sponsored research projects in universities, the present system of paying for indirect costs is relatively recent.[11] In 1946, NIH decided not to pay any indirect costs. In the wake of negative reactions from universities, it grudgingly changed its policy to allow indirect cost recovery, but to cap the payments at 8 percent of direct costs, which matched the maximum rate permitted by the Office of Naval Research (ONR). (Virtually all universities negotiate their cost reimbursement methods with either NIH or ONR.)

Shortly thereafter, ONR devised a set of principles for calculating allowable indirect costs. In 1958, these principles evolved into the first version of Circular A-21, the general guidelines for university cost accounting promulgated then by the Bureau of the Budget and now managed by its successor agency, OMB.

Congress became directly involved in setting indirect cost rates in 1958 by passing legislation that capped the indirect cost rate at 15 percent. In 1963, Congress raised the cap to 20 percent. In 1965, a government commission reported that the 20 percent cap was insufficient to cover research costs. It recommended that indirect costs, like direct costs, be reimbursed on the basis of the costs actually experienced instead of an arbitrary cap. In 1966, Congress removed the cap but insisted that universities share in the cost of federally sponsored research. Circular A-21 was revised to implement this legislation.

After the new policy was put in place, indirect cost rates began a slow but inexorable climb upward, reaching an average rate of nearly 50 percent by the 1990s. By 1980, indirect cost rates had resurfaced as a controversial policy issue, and several attempts were made to cap either the overall rate or components of it. All of these proposals were rejected at some point; indeed, in 1986 Congress passed legislation that removed mandatory cost sharing by universities. Not until 1991 did OMB finally impose a cap of 26 percent on the rate for indirect administrative costs.

Although OMB oversees the cost accounting practices employed by universities, implementation of OMB's policies varies among agencies, and within an agency, among universities. Ultimately, the procedures for estimating and auditing costs are negotiated individually with each university through its "lead agency" (NIH or ONR). Hence, no general description can be entirely accurate without resorting to a mind-boggling array of details and exceptions. Nevertheless, some basic features are common to almost all cases.[12]

The basic function of the cost accounting system is to define a set of final cost objectives, or products that the university can be viewed as producing, and then to assign every dollar of cost incurred by the university to one and only one of these cost objectives. Under such a system, the university's total costs equal the sum of the costs of producing individual products. The accounting systems used by universities recognize each federally supported research project as a separate cost objective or product. Other activities and research projects not supported by federal research grants are also recognized as separate final cost objectives. As a result, every dollar of cost is allocated either to a particular federally sponsored research project or to some other final cost objective.

The accounting system is quite different for direct and indirect costs. Direct costs are easily and unambiguously broken down into components that are used to support only one final cost objective. Indirect costs are grouped into various categories, called pools, and allocated to final cost objectives using a specific formula.

Though some costs clearly are either direct or indirect, typically a broad mass of costs could be treated either way, depending on the standards used to define which costs can easily and unambiguously be broken down into components that support only one objective. In practice, the federal government and universities have developed somewhat arbitrary distinctions for separating direct and indirect costs. Typically, direct costs include the time nonfaculty research personnel spend working on the project; expendable materials and supplies used in carrying out research; clerical and administrative personnel assigned primarily to the project; travel and conferences for research personnel; and equipment acquired for use on the project, rather than for supporting many projects.

Indirect costs are divided into several general categories: depreciation, operation, and maintenance of buildings and equipment; general and departmental administration (including accounting and auditing functions); libraries; and student services (because students work as research assistants on federally sponsored projects). Clerical and administrative personnel who work on several projects usually are treated as part of indirect administrative costs, even though it is technically possible to require them to keep records indicating how they spent their time. Likewise, utility expenses are treated as part of building operation costs, even though it would be feasible to meter usage in research labs.

The amount of overhead allocated to any particular federally sponsored project is determined as follows. Overhead costs are divided into various functional pools. For each pool, detailed studies are performed periodically to determine the fraction of each pool allocated to federal research projects. A costing study for a particular pool is typically undertaken only once every few years, with the results then used for allocating indirect costs until a new study is performed. These studies are often expensive and detailed. They involve extensive data collection and complex algebraic calculations, which tend to give them a patina of objectivity and technical respectability. In fact, it is difficult to think of a reason for carrying out these calculations other than to give the results this patina of scientific precision. Most of these costs are joint costs of many if not all university activities, making a nonarbitrary attribution of these costs among activities impossible. To emphasize our view of the nature of these calculations, we refer to them as the PCBA (Precisely Calculated But Arbitrary) fractions.

For example, the fraction of library costs allocated to federal grants is often determined by conducting surveys. People who enter a library are asked whether they made that particular trip to perform federally sponsored research. In similar fashion, the fraction of the cost of faculty office space and laboratories allocated to federal grants is typically determined by asking a faculty member (or whoever else is present when the surveyor arrives) what fraction of the total activity in the office or lab is devoted to federally sponsored research, as opposed to other research, teaching, or administration.

These questions presuppose that the time spent on federally sponsored research is clearly separable from the time spent on other activities. For example, the concept of a specific federally sponsored research project is often arbitrary, as all of the work directed by a faculty member may be closely related and supported by several sources. Likewise, the time a faculty member spends explaining a research project to a student research assistant, or teaching the student how to use laboratory equipment, is both research and education. Our experience is that the responses to these surveys about how time and space are allocated to federally sponsored research vary widely because people interpret questions differently when they are asked to make arbitrary allocations among joint activities.

Given the PCBA fractions that are determined as we have described, overhead costs are allocated to federal research projects according to the following procedure. The PCBA fraction for a particular overhead pool is multiplied by the total costs in that pool. The costs so allocated from each pool are added to determine the total amount of overhead costs allocated to federal research grants. This total is allocated across federal grants in proportion to the direct costs (excluding equipment costs) charged to each grant.

Grant awards are based on projected accounting costs. To project overhead costs on government grants, the university (in conjunction with the federal government) must estimate the university's total overhead costs and the direct costs to be charged to federal grants. The ratio of estimated total overhead costs for federal research to estimated direct costs of government grants, after some exclusions, is than calculated to create a projected overhead rate.[13] When submitting individual federal grants, the university multiplies the eligible direct costs by the projected overhead rate to determine a projected overhead cost for the contract.

An important characteristic of the reimbursement process for both direct and indirect costs is that though award amounts are based on projected accounting costs, the university is ultimately allowed to keep this money only if audited accounting costs are equal to or greater than the amounts awarded. Federal contract awards are thus ultimately based on ex post accounting costs.

The university and its principal investigators maintain close control over direct costs and have considerable latitude in transferring expenditures among categories of direct costs. Typically there is no large discrepancy between the amount awarded and the amount spent. Any discrepancies that do occur are settled on a grant-by-grant basis. The university and principal investigators have much less control over whether actual overhead accounting costs equal the amount of indirect cost recovery, because indirect cost recovery depends on factors such as the university's overall level of government research awards and the overall level of overhead costs. In the case of indirect costs, discrepancies are settled on an aggregate basis for an entire year's contracts. Discrepancies in any one year usually are corrected by adjusting aggregate overhead payments in subsequent years, although the government occasionally insists that the university pay its excess collections immediately.

For both direct and indirect costs, the federal government classifies certain types of costs as unallowable. These items must not be included in cost calculations for purposes of determining federal reimbursement. Unallowable costs fall into four categories.

The first category, which receives all of the public attention because of the potential for scandal, consists of costs viewed as being extravagant or unnecessary. Examples would include certain types of entertainment expenses, first-class airfares, and the like. The detection of these types of unallowable costs has generated great public controversy, but in reality these rules prevent the reimbursement of only a handful of easily identifiable types of expenditures and are financially insignificant. As long as the expenditure is not one of these forbidden types, it is allowable. For example, the cost of a new research facility may be extravagant because of an unnecessarily expensive architectural design or the use of expensive building materials, or a library may buy many obscure journals that are not read; the rules on allowability of costs are not designed to discover this type of waste. In practice, then, the requirement that expenditures not be unnecessary is a minimal and unimportant restriction.

The second category of unallowable costs consists of facilities that have been paid for by the federal government. For example, if a university receives a government grant to construct a building, the depreciation of that building is not included in the indirect cost pool. In addition, state universities are generally less aggressive in collecting indirect costs on facilities built from state government funds.[14] These practices are financially far more significant than the disallowances of the first type. Average indirect cost rates are about ten percentage points lower for public than for private universities.[15]

Many federal agencies, including some NSF programs, will not pay any fraction of the academic-year salaries of full-time faculty performing the research, although these agencies will pay summer salary supplements.[16] The exclusion of faculty salaries from many research grants starkly demonstrates that the federal system for paying for university research is clearly not "full cost reimbursement."

Finally, beginning in about 1990, the federal government began to adopt a new approach for disallowing costs, in response to a substantial increase in indirect cost rates during the 1970s and especially the 1980s. In general, the government has increased the stringency of many accounting and audit procedures. Federal agencies have become more forceful in bilateral negotiations about the methods for allocating indirect cost pools as well as the final rate, especially with the large private universities that charge the highest rates.[17] The end result is that an increasing fraction of the accounting costs derived from the procedures authorized by the government are not reimbursed even though they are, in principle and by prior agreement, reimbursable. Two significant examples of tougher policies that override the detailed rules for calculating indirect costs are the cap on the component of the indirect cost rate that covers administrative costs, and the termination of automatic carryforward of the underrecovery of authorized indirect costs through increments to indirect costs rates in subsequent years. These changes are widening the gap between the accounting costs of federally sponsored research and the amount actually paid by the government.

The Effects of the Present System

The cost reimbursement approach to R&D grants begins with adapting tools invented for other purposes toward addressing the problem of establishing mutual obligations between contracting parties. Accounting was invented to assist firms in monitoring their own performance. It is nontrivial and interesting only because firms typically are sufficiently complex that managers are uncertain about precisely how their resources are used and whether a particular use of resources is profitable. Only then is a formal, costly method of systematically measuring resource use helpful to managers. The original and still primary purpose of accounting systems is to assist managers of an organization in carrying out their jobs effectively.[18]

Because an accounting system must incorporate fundamentally arbitrary methods of allocating the unallocatable and measuring the unmeasurable, it is an inherently imperfect mechanism to measure progress toward an organization's goals. If managers use accounting system to make decisions, employees have an incentive to alter their behavior in ways that enhance their performance strictly as measured by the accounting system. Managers therefore use accounting systems as only one of many tools to measure employee productivity and to sharpen employee incentives to maximize their contribution to the organization's objectives.

To use accounting and auditing procedures to govern transactions between organizations creates new incentive problems of this same type. Now the managers of the organization have an incentive to adjust their operations to maximize reimbursement that they receive under the accounting rules, which in turn are only imperfectly aligned with the goals of the sponsor. In principle, government contract officers could respond to this problem by creating additional methods for monitoring contractors and sharpening their incentives, but they are handicapped in doing so for two reasons.

Government does not have certain techniques for creating incentives for university managers, including bonuses, stock options, and regular performance reviews. Indeed, if it had such tools, the managers would be government workers, not managers of an independent organization, and the purpose of decentralized procurement would be defeated.

In addition, because universities derive revenue from many sources other than a government agency that sponsors research, the contract officer cannot influence the form of contracts and other transaction arrangements between the university and other entities. As a result, the government cannot control distorting incentives that are created by differences in the formal relationships between a university and each of its customers. Accounting procedures that might be minimally distorting if they were uniformly applied to all sources of revenue can become uncorrectably distorting if different accounting methods are used for governing relations with different organizations.[19]

After describing the main incentives created by the current system and arguing that the general approach taken is a reasonable response to the nature of the government's contracting problem, we discuss some of the problems created by the system as it stands. A useful place to begin is to discuss the notion of incremental cost in greater detail.

Incremental Cost

Some federal officials have proposed that universities should receive, at most, the incremental cost of a research project to the university and that even these costs should possibly be shared.[20] To understand the meaning and effect of these proposals requires a detailed understanding of the concept of the incremental and nonincremental costs of research projects.

The incremental cost of an activity is the extra cost incurred by undertaking it, holding all other activities constant. Incremental cost is, by definition, the minimum amount that an organization would have to be paid to be willing to undertake an activity if no funds were available from other sources. Two particular features of the concept of incremental cost and how it applies to research projects undertaken by universities are especially important: the relevant time horizon, and the confounding effect of synergies (or complementarities).

The incremental cost of a research project generally depends on the duration of the plan being considered. In general, incremental cost is larger for longer time periods. For a short time frame, the university may have sunk resources in productive facilities that have no alternate uses, while for long time frames fewer of these decisions will have been made. Economists often speak of two notional time horizons: the short run, in which significant sunk expenditures have been incurred; and the long run, in which investments in all sunk expenditures must be replaced.

For research projects, we might think of the short run as lasting a few years and the long run as lasting a decade or more. The short-run incremental cost of a research project would include costs for some equipment, materials, and supplies not yet purchased as well as some salaries. However, certain salaries would not be part of short-term incremental cost because the university would not fire personnel immediately if the loss of grant support were considered temporary, or if long-term employment contracts (such as academic tenure) prevent it from doing so. Similarly, the university may have purchased certain equipment that would be used on the project, trained certain personnel, and built and recently refurbished the building that would house the project. Finally, the administrative superstructure may have been designed to support a certain level of grant activity and might not be able to adjust instantaneously. To the extent that administrative costs cannot vary with the level of grant activity, they would not be included in short-term incremental cost.

In the long run, most costs become part of incremental costs to the extent that they would adjust to changes in activity level. If the loss of research grants were permanent, the university might not replace or renovate an obsolete building that houses research facilities and might make long-term adjustments in the size of its faculty and administration. These costs are incremental in the long run.

The second feature of incremental cost is that, for any organization pursuing multiple activities, the incremental cost of a group of activities considered as a whole is likely to be larger than the sum of the incremental cost of each activity considered separately. When productive synergies exist between activities (such synergies are called economies of scale or scope), these activities have joint costs.[21] These joint costs are not incremental with respect to any single activity but are nonetheless incremental with respect to all joint activities considered together.

To illustrate the significance of this point, suppose that we calculate the incremental cost of each of a university's federally funded research projects. That is, for each project, we determine the costs that could be avoided if that project were not undertaken (but if all other activities of the university, including all other federally funded research projects, were). All of these costs added together are the total incremental costs of federally funded research projects. We can now view all of the university's federally funded research projects as a single activity and calculate the incremental cost of this activity. This is the incremental cost of all federally funded research. The latter number is virtually always larger than the former. That is, the sum of the incremental cost of all federally funded projects is less than the incremental cost of all federally sponsored research.

The reason for this difference is that federally sponsored research projects have synergies. A university can take advantage of the fact that it has multiple research projects to lower its costs of conducting each project. For example, the university may use a piece of equipment on several projects. If only one project were canceled, the university would still need to purchase the equipment to conduct the remaining projects. The cost of the equipment is therefore not an incremental cost of any specific project. If the university canceled all projects, it would then no longer need to purchase the equipment, so the equipment cost is incremental to all projects considered together. One can make similar arguments about buildings, faculty, graduate research assistants, libraries, and university administration.

To guarantee that a university is paid enough to be willing to undertake federally sponsored research, the university must receive at least the long-term incremental cost of all federal research. If the government only pays short-term marginal cost, the university can maintain its research level for a few years. However, it cannot do so in the long run unless it finds additional funds to maintain the university's capital investments, research faculty, and administrative support system. Even paying the long-term incremental cost for each project will be insufficient to maintain the university's ability to undertake such projects, because the shared costs will not be reimbursed. The incremental cost of a single project may be low because many costs are incurred jointly with other federally sponsored activities. However, these joint costs must be paid by someone if a university is to undertake federal research.

Just as it is folly to pretend that indirect costs do not have to be paid because they are not incremental with respect to any specific project, it is equally foolish to pretend that a particular project is a financial albatross if it does not pay as high an indirect cost rate as other projects. From a financial standpoint, the university's financial status and the viability of its other activities are unaffected by the presence or absence of an activity for which the university is paid its long-term incremental cost. Consequently, a university is unambiguously better off financially if it accepts a grant that pays more than the long-term incremental cost of the new research that the grant supports and that does not substitute for a grant that pays a higher indirect cost rate.

Moreover, if the university accepts a new grant that pays a lower indirect cost rate than is paid by the federal government, the federal government also benefits! The reason for this is that if a new research activity supported by a grant makes any contribution, however small, to pay for the fixed indirect costs of the university, the amount of overhead charged to the government in the future will be less. Whereas some claim that a project is being subsidized if it generates less indirect cost recovery than the federal rate, in reality *all* research sponsors are better off (and *no* project is subsidized) if every grant includes some payment in excess of the incremental cost of the project.

Desirable Features of the Current System

The general approach of the current system is a reasonable response to the nature of the government's contracting problem. It responds to the measurement problems of contracting for research, and, by overcompensating universities for federally sponsored research, it gives universities an incentive to become strong research institutions. The complete argument for the current system is fourfold.

1. COST-BASED CONTRACTS MAKE SENSE FOR DIRECT COSTS BUT NOT INDIRECT COSTS. Because output is intangible and uncertain, government uses direct costs as the best available description of the research project that the university and government agree will be undertaken. Direct costs do bear a close relationship to the nature of the research undertaken, so they are not seriously misleading as an indicator of the product emanating from a research grant. Moreover, because direct costs are closely associated with the research undertaken, government program officers and peer reviewers can do some crude monitoring of the reasonableness of the expenditures, given the proposed research. With respect to

direct costs, there seems to be no real alternative to cost-based contracting.

For indirect costs, the amount charged to a project bears no close relationship to the proposed research, and its reasonableness cannot be monitored easily. Cost-based contracting for indirect costs is substantially more of a problem than cost-based contracts for direct costs.

2. THE ACCOUNTING COSTS OF FEDERALLY SPONSORED RESEARCH PROBABLY EXCEED THE LONG-TERM INCREMENTAL COST OF THIS RE-SEARCH. The accounting cost of all federally funded research at a university probably exceeds the long-term incremental cost of performing all federally funded research. That is, universities have been earning a markup over the incremental cost on federally funded research. Most direct costs are probably incremental in the long run, and the government has largely reimbursed nearly all of these. However, in some cases the indirect costs charged to federally sponsored research are clearly not incremental with respect to these projects. By reimbursing these costs, the federal government has thus provided reimbursement greater than incremental cost.

Some indirect costs charged to the government are not incremental with respect to federally sponsored research because of complementarities among federally funded research projects, other research, education, and other university activities (most notably health care services, as discussed in chapter 6). Complementarities cause these indirect costs not to be incremental to any activity. The incremental cost concept here is based on retaining the quantity and quality of all other activities, including education, research, and health care. To retain the same quality of these activities, universities still would be required to have extensive laboratory facilities, to involve students in research, and to have accounting procedures in place that enabled accounting for expenditures from other grants and contracts.

How much of federal indirect cost is incremental is difficult to say. For most research universities, most expenditures on plant and equipment are financed by private donors and state governments. For libraries and administration, a considerable part of physical investment and personnel would need to be present in any case to support other activities of the university. As a result, a substantial portion of building depreciation, library costs, and administrative expenses are not incremental to federally sponsored research. For private research universities these categories account for at least 33 percent (and frequently more) of all overhead costs, and about 30 percent of total grant awards goes toward recovery of indirect costs. Private research universities therefore receive a markup of at least 10 percent, and perhaps more, over the total incremental costs of federal research.

3. PAYMENTS IN EXCESS OF LONG-TERM INCREMENTAL COSTS SERVE A USEFUL FUNCTION FOR THE FEDERAL GOVERNMENT AND BENEFIT THE UNIVERSITY AS WELL. Retaining a markup over incremental cost performs a desirable and necessary function. A markup on numerous grants creates a prize that rewards a university for maintaining a strong research environment. As we have argued, it is naive to think that universities are somehow automatically programmed to want to produce high-quality scientific research. The prospect of a large prize that can be used to support other university activities creates a substantial incentive to undertake high-quality research. Many faculty, students, and administrators have no direct interest in the science and engineering fields that account for virtually all federal support for university research. In the absence of a broader university stake in federal grants, these members of the university community have no reason to foster these fields. The markup on grants gives the entire community an incentive to keep its scientists and engineers competitive for future research grants.

4. THE PRESENT MARKUP IN GRANT AWARDS OVER LONG-TERM INCREMENTAL COST IS A RELATIVELY INEXPENSIVE WAY TO ACHIEVE THESE BENEFITS. Seemingly the more difficult part of the argument is to explain why paying a markup of 10 percent does not cost the federal government much. One reason that the markup is not expensive is that the federal government probably values the other outputs of the university (and so wants to retain the quality and scope of university activities). Consequently, the markup is

simply an indirect form of procurement. Undoubtedly some of the markup goes to pay for projects that the university values highly but that the federal government does not. However, a university's preferences are not likely to be completely in conflict with those of the federal government. Thus, the research, education, and health care arising from the markup are also of some value to the federal government, which reduces the net effective cost of the markup to government.

In addition, if the federal government did not include some payment for the nonincremental indirect costs of the university in the overhead rate on grants, it eventually would have to find another way to pay for them if it wanted research universities to survive at their present quality and quantity of research. Although some indirect costs may not be incremental with respect to any single activity, they somehow must be paid. If no one pays for them, and if universities are not leaving significant opportunities for revenue unexploited, then the university must generate the funds to pay these costs by eliminating or reducing the quality of other activities. Some of the markup on federal research grants therefore simply goes to support overhead costs that the government would have to find some other way to pay for if it did not pay markups on federal research grants.

Problems with the Current System

The main undesirable feature of the current cost reimbursement system is that it adds to the total cost of federally sponsored research in at least three ways.

1. THE SYSTEM IS UNNECESSARILY COSTLY. Maintaining the system of accounts and audits to implement cost reimbursement is itself a costly procedure, but the product of this process is indirect cost recovery rates that are broadly similar across categories of universities. Table 5-1 contains the indirect cost rates at about seventy universities. Because the sample is based on the universities that are most successful in obtaining grants from NIH, a few otherwise strong institutions that have no medical school and are not leaders in biology (for example, Princeton) are excluded,

Table 5-1. Indirect Cost Rates at Selected Universities, 1992

University	Rate	University	Rate	University	Rate
Alabama-Birmingham	.42	George Washington	.48	North Carolina	.445
Arizona	.484	Medical	.60	Northwestern	.51
Baylor Medical	.45	Georgetown	.59	Ohio State	.45
Boston U.	.73	Harvard	.68	Penn	.65
Brandeis	.59	Medical	.77	Penn State	.444
Brown	.68	Public Health	.54	Pittsburgh	.43
Caltech	.58	Illinois-Chicago	.56	Purdue	.49
Calif.—Berkeley	.49	Illinois-Urbana/Champaign	.517	Rochester	.57
Calif.—Davis	.412	Indiana	.49	Rockefeller	.68
Calif.—Irvine	.475	Indiana/Purdue	.49	Rutgers	.64
Calif.—Los Angeles	.48	Iowa	.41	St. Louis	.44
Calif.—San Diego	.49	Johns Hopkins	.64	Southern California	.63
Calif.—San Francisco	.385	Kansas Medical	.47	Stanford	.74
Case Western Reserve	.51	Kentucky	.49	SUNY-Buffalo	.527
Chicago	.65	LSU Medical	.39	SUNY-Stony Brook	.524
Colorado	.418	MIT	.62	Temple	.61
Medical	.45	Maryland-Baltimore Co.	.52	Texas-Austin	.47
Colorado State	.45	Mass. Medical	.65	Tufts	.67
Columbia	.741	Miami Medical	.54	Utah	.475

Cornell public	.57	Michigan	.59	Vanderbilt	.61
Private	.70	Michigan State	.45	Vermont	.526
Medical	.50	Minnesota	.44	Virginia	.52
Dartmouth	.50	Missouri	.38	Virginia Commonwealth	.52
Duke	.50	Medical	.315	Washington	.51
Emory	.52	NYU	.51	Wash. U.	.60
Florida	.45	Medical	.635	Wisconsin	.44
				Yale	.68

Source: Health and Human Services Working Group on the Costs of Research, *Management of Research. Costs: Indirect Costs* (May 1992), appendix III.

whereas a few state universities that are not research universities but have a strong medical school are included.

As is apparent from table 5-1, indirect cost rates do differ among universities, but are quite similar in peer groups. For example, ten leading private research universities (Caltech, Chicago, Columbia, Cornell, Harvard, Johns Hopkins, MIT, Pennsylvania, Stanford, and Yale), based on amounts of support and general prestige, had an average indirect cost rate of 67 percent in 1992, excluding separate rates for medical schools. Six of the ten had rates within three percentage points of the average. Likewise, twelve leading public universities (five University of California campuses except San Francisco [essentially a medical school], Illinois, Michigan, Minnesota, Penn State, Texas, Washington, and Wisconsin) had an average indirect cost rate of 48 percent. These universities are somewhat more dispersed, with six of twelve being within three percentage points of the average.

Of course, small differences in indirect costs can make a difference in grant revenues. For the top twenty-five research universities, annual revenues from the direct costs of sponsored research (excluding the items that are not eligible for indirect cost recovery) were in the range of $100 million to $200 million in 1994, the last year for which complete data are available.[22] If eligible direct cost revenue is $100 million to $200 million, a swing of five percentage points in the indirect cost rate would produce a swing in revenues of $5 million to $10 million. However, a university with this volume of research would have total revenues of several times the amount of its federal research support, so this change in most cases would be much less than a year's growth in income.

Despite producing broadly similar results, research-intensive universities spend substantial sums on the administrative apparatus that supports accounting and auditing indirect costs. We do not know precisely how much administrative cost is associated with estimating indirect costs. What is known is that indirect costs account for about 30 percent (about $3 billion) of sponsored research payments from the federal government, and that about 20 percent of indirect costs (more than $500 million) is accounted for by the administrative categories that include accounting, auditing, and monitoring grants.[23] Our experience at our own universities is that the proportion of administrative effort associated with the indirect costs of sponsored research is high. A large part of the negotiations with the government about accounting and auditing practices deal with indirect costs, and some "special studies" to document particular components of indirect costs run in the millions of dollars.

2. THE SYSTEM DOES NOT REWARD EFFICIENCY.   Cost reimbursement contracting provides little direct incentive for universities to manage indirect costs efficiently. Of course, an indirect incentive to manage costs efficiently is created by the fact that universities compete for grants, and the cost of performing the research is one factor that sponsoring agencies consider. Furthermore, at least for direct costs, agencies and peer review panels attempt to make some broad determination of whether costs are reasonable. However, these factors do not provide as strong an incentive to minimize indirect costs because program officers and peer reviewers have no way of knowing whether indirect costs are reasonable, and no means of controlling these costs even if they believe the rates are too high. Moreover, negotiations over rates and auditing systems do not focus on whether expenditures were efficient— just on whether they were made for the purpose stated.

3. THE SYSTEM DISTORTS UNIVERSITY MANAGEMENT.   The particular practice of basing overhead reimbursement on a university's own accounting estimates of overhead costs creates serious and systematic incentives for universities to distort the way they conduct their activities to maximize the amount of overhead allocated to government contracts—and that government grants will pay for.

Suppose that one type of research requires facilities that are more expensive than classrooms, while another type of research requires only the least expensive type of facility. In this case, the university can maximize indirect cost recovery by bundling low-cost research with classrooms and separating high-cost research from educational spaces, even if this arrangement is inefficient. The high-cost research facilities then will be fully reimbursed, whereas the reimbursement for low-cost research facilities will be a weighted average of the true costs and the (higher) cost of classrooms.

Typically, research labs do have higher construction, maintenance, and operating costs than most other space. As a result, indirect cost accounting creates an incentive for universities to physically separate high-cost facilities with a substantial volume of federally sponsored research. This practice reduces the efficiency of university operations by inhibiting collaborative interaction across these physical boundaries and creating unnatural barriers between research and other activities, notably education, health care, and other community service activities. For example, indirect cost recovery procedures provide a disincentive for universities to make educational uses of research facilities that are used for federally sponsored projects, and to allow students to work in labs for academic credit rather than as research assistants.

Another example of a socially destructive distortion is the incentive that indirect cost recovery creates for the university to wall itself off from its surrounding community. Consider the case of a research library. Research universities subscribe to a long list of arcane (and very expensive) technical journals. If a university adopts the socially desirable policy of allowing members of the surrounding community to use its library, the indirect cost audit will measure that a lower fraction of use is accounted for by sponsored research and so cut the fraction of library costs that can be recovered as part of overhead. Quite rationally, the university is likely to make its research library off limits to outsiders to increase its total grant payments from the government.

The Case for Prospective Reimbursement

The main lesson of the preceding section is that indirect cost recovery for federal research grants is a procedure that allows universities to set a markup over the incremental costs of federal research. This markup rewards universities for committing resources to areas of research that have high federal priority and for creating an environment that supports and fosters high-quality research. Furthermore, as long as the purposes of federal support for university research extend beyond simply supporting the particular projects that receive awards, providing some excess of revenues over incremental costs is necessary.

Given this understanding of the economic role of overhead reimbursement, the current method of establishing markups is seriously flawed. The goals in choosing a markup are to cover all incremental costs and to provide an incentive for universities to want to win these awards. In doing so, universities can pay for other activities that they value and, for the most part, policymakers want as well. Perhaps a markup approximately the same as a university's own overhead rate provides roughly the correct incentive, but no theory predicts that current rates, or any others, are somehow precisely correct. In any case, variation in the magnitude of the markup among similar universities appears to have no justification in either economic analysis or public policy. Because overhead rates do not vary dramatically within broad classes of universities (for example, public versus private, or rank in the quality of education and research), essentially the same incentive could be created by using prospective benchmark standards for overhead rates.

The concept of an indirect cost benchmark is to apply the same fixed markup rate for overhead costs to each type of university, based on a thorough government audit of overhead at a sample of peer universities. Benchmarks would be established by undertaking intensive, government-financed audits of a few universities. Universities would no longer be required to retain existing accounting systems for allocating indirect cost pools, to justify the amount recovered, or to undertake regular audits to authenticate that their indirect cost recovery was justified. Instead, they would simply have to maintain sufficiently transparent records that they could support a federal audit should they be selected as one of the universities audited to establish the next benchmark rate. The indirect cost rates derived from these audits would be fixed for several years, requiring the government to conduct only a few infrequent audits and giving universities a stable rate on which to base long-term capital expenditure plans and annual budgeting. The results of the audits would not be used to adjust any past indirect cost recovery for any university, including those audited. The total amount of indirect cost recovery by a particular university would bear no relationship to its actual indirect costs. It would instead be determined by the average proportion of indirect costs of all universities and its own success in winning awards.

The procedure for establishing nationwide indirect cost recovery rates must include a method for categorizing universities. One approach, which minimizes the redistribution of indirect cost recovery among universities, would lump together groups of universities that now have similar rates and status. The types of distinctions that would serve this purpose are public versus private status, region, and rank in terms of research quality. This approach requires an objective mechanism for classifying universities that allows periodic reclassification to reflect changes in status. The interests of the federal government dictate that if a university undertakes a program to improve its faculty and research facilities and improves its ranking, it should be able to recover the rate given to its new peer group, not the past one.

A second approach would remove some of the rate difference in the present system. For example, the present practice of different reimbursement rates for public and private universities is difficult to defend if the point of indirect cost recovery is to generate a financial incentive to invest in research of interest to the government. The observation that some state governments return indirect cost recovery to the treasury is a superficial reason not to pay these universities the full amount of indirect cost recovery, for doing so would give the state government a greater incentive to invest in university facilities. Moreover, if a state persistently just keeps indirect cost recovery for other purposes, its university will deteriorate—and so will see its grant income (and indirect cost recovery) decline.

Recent changes in federal policies regarding indirect costs represent a first step in rationalizing indirect cost recovery. The cap on university administrative costs is a ubiquitous rate for one overhead category, and negotiated rates not strictly tied to indirect cost accounts move in the direction of simply setting a markup over direct costs. Both have the advantage of attenuating the relationship between incurring a cost and receiving a payment, counteracting to some extent the incentive not to control costs.

Unfortunately, these changes as implemented have substantial disadvantages. They still are based on complex accounting and auditing processes, and universities are still required to provide ex post justification for the costs that they recover, even if actual costs substantially exceed the caps.[24] In addition, negotiated rates are determined separately for each university, even though the outcome of the process is roughly similar in each case. These negotiations consume a great deal of administrative effort in universities as well as the government. They serve no real purpose once one has abandoned the idea that rates are calculated on the basis of the principle of cost reimbursement.

The better way to implement the cap on administrative costs would be to adopt a flat rate for each peer group of universities and to relieve them of the responsibility for auditing these costs. This approach was proposed in 1988 by a panel organized by the American Association of Universities, under the leadership of Cornelius J. Pings, then the provost of the University of Southern California and now the head of AAU.[25] The Pings report found that the aggregate rate for all administrative costs varied only slightly among universities, so that adopting one rate for all would cause little disruption. The report also recommended "threshold" rates for libraries and student services that a university could adopt without providing proof by audit that actual expenditures matched or exceeded the flat rate.

The Pings recommendations remain a far better approach than the current system, and an excellent first step toward eliminating the present system. Certainly a transition period in which universities could retain some features of the present system would ease the adjustment for schools with unusually high rates for their peer group—although, as explained above, the magnitude of the required adjustment is a small fraction of total revenues for even the outliers. In any case, the government's response to the Pings report—to cap administrative costs but retain the auditing requirements and the rate negotiation process—ignores the single most important feature of the proposal: fixing a benchmark rate that is not likely to be affected by the cost experience of a single university, thus encouraging efficient administration.

Our proposal goes beyond the Pings report to recommend a flat rate for the indirect costs of buildings and equipment within each peer group of universities. Universities have steadfastly opposed this approach. They argue that, unlike administrative costs, building and equipment costs can legitimately differ quite a bit among universities within the same peer group because of differences in the relative amounts of different types of research each university undertakes. In theory, this observation is correct, but it is not conclusive.

As a practical matter, except for single-purpose medical schools and universities in which only the medical school receives a significant amount of federal research support, research universities tend not to be highly specialized in particular areas of science or engineering. Except for the differences between public and private universities and among regions resulting from differences in utility and construction costs, the unexplained variance in this component of indirect costs apparently is rather small.[26] Moreover, if some universities did respond to a ubiquitous flat rate by specializing in fields that require little capital investment, the government could develop a peer group of specialized institutions that had its own rate. Furthermore, if benchmarking were adopted, provisions for special exemptions to retain the old system either permanently or during a transition could be made available for the few hard cases. The existing variation among universities thus falls into the category of a moderately interesting problem that can be solved, rather than an inequity so immense that it makes the proposal unattractive.

Perhaps a more likely reason for resistance to benchmarking for buildings and equipment is that, unlike administrative costs, universities do not want to face an incentive to control these expenditures. Recall that the fundamental problem in keeping these costs reasonable is knowing whether they are necessary and efficient. Universities probably do not serve the objectives of faculty or top management by having a larger staff than they need for accounting and auditing; however, these groups may enjoy gold-plated buildings. Moreover, excessive expenditures on buildings but not on administration are typically financed from new and separate university funds (donors, state construction budgets). This enables the university to collect twice for building costs (the second time through indirect cost recovery). By contrast, because donors are unlikely to endow administrative costs, universities collect the administrative costs of federal grants only once. Universities therefore have a much stronger incentive to reject benchmarking for facilities costs than for administrative ones.

A benchmark system for all components of indirect cost recovery has five important features that merit a summary.

First, the proposed system would continue to fulfill its main functions: providing a prize to universities for winning research grants, and paying for some of the nonincremental overhead costs necessary to support all university activities. Because overhead rates within broad categories of universities do not vary greatly, this objective could be accomplished without a sudden, massive redistribution of grant revenue.

Benchmarking indirect costs also reduces accounting and auditing requirements, providing an opportunity for considerable cost savings. Increasingly stringent accounting rules and intensive audits have caused a dramatic increase in administrative indirect costs. Part of administrative overhead is because of accounting, auditing, negotiating, and even litigating indirect costs.

A third feature is that, under a benchmarking system, universities would experience a new and potentially powerful incentive to eliminate excessive overhead expenditures. Under the current system, when a university incurs extra overhead expenditures for any allowable cost, it creates a basis for requesting a higher reimbursement rate from the federal government. Under a benchmark system, universities have an incentive to economize on indirect costs. This in turn maximizes the difference between reimbursements and actual costs, which is the markup that can be spent on other priorities. Incentive prizes created by markups are valuable; they encourage universities to incur overhead expenditures that increase the ability of the university to obtain research grants, but discourage spending on frills.

In addition, the leverage that the federal government can exercise over universities about how they spend on indirect costs is minimal. The government has attempted to control some elements of indirect costs by capping them, by negotiating rates that are lower than the rates justified by the accounting procedures that the government requires, and by insisting that some funds from indirect cost recovery be spent in the same cost category. But this interventionist approach is procedurally costly. Moreover, direct government oversight is not likely to have much effect on the propensity of a university to make extravagant and wasteful expenditures. This is not because universities are so adeptly managed, but because the government has no effective means for using indirect cost accounting to improve the quality of university management. Benchmarking replaces ineffective auditing procedures with much more effective direct incentives.

Finally, the current system creates a serious and systematic set of incentives for universities to distort the way they conduct their research and other activities to maximize the amount of overhead that government will pay. Under benchmarking, all of these distortions would vanish.

Conclusions

The rationale for a system of cost reimbursement for the direct costs of university research grants is easy to comprehend. Research projects are likely to vary enormously in cost, depending on the number of personnel involved, the equipment needed, and so on. One would be hard put to justify a method for reimbursing direct costs of a research grant that did not explicitly deal with differences in resources committed to, say, research projects in abstract mathematics versus high-energy physics. To induce universities to strike a proper balance between inexpensive and expensive projects (that is, not to specialize in mathematics while closing down laboratory sciences), the size of a grant must reflect its direct costs. Insisting that a university must be able to prove that the direct cost award was actually spent as promised is also prudent, given that the research output from a grant cannot be objectively specified in advance or accurately measured after the project is completed.

As a result, a cost reimbursement system for direct costs has considerable merit. It places restrictions on the uses of the grant by both the university and investigator. Yet it does not severely restrict the freedom with which the investigator manages the project, including selecting the specific research tasks to be carried out. Even though an elaborate accounting system for measuring direct costs may be expensive, it is likely to have significant advantages that would be difficult to match under any alternative.

A system of indirect cost reimbursement based on a university's own accounting costs is much more difficult to defend. Indirect cost recovery is best conceptualized as a procedure for allowing universities to set a markup over direct costs. This markup rewards universities for supporting and fostering high-quality research in areas the federal government chooses to support, reimburses universities for part of the overhead costs that support all of their activities, and gives them a little extra for fostering other activities that do not receive federal grants.

Because actual overhead rates do not vary a great deal within each broad class of universities, reimbursing overhead according to benchmark rates could accomplish the same desirable functions. Prospective reimbursement also would eliminate costly accounting and auditing requirements, provide universities with much greater incentives to manage their own overhead costs prudently, and remove a number of other distortions caused by retrospective cost-based reimbursement of overhead. For all these reasons, we recommend that the federal government develop a system of grant awards for universities that makes far more extensive use of benchmarking.

Endnotes

1. In addition to project grants, the federal government also supports university research through institutional grants, contracts with universities to manage national labs, and payments to university medical centers for health services that exceed their costs. This chapter focuses exclusively on research grants because they are an extremely important activity for research universities and because they raise quite different contracting problems than the other two forms of federal support.

2. The term "full cost reimbursement" is misleading for two reasons. First, the federal government makes various costs nonreimbursable, even if they are truly costs of performing the research. In addition, in an environment with joint costs, "the" cost of a project cannot be defined unambiguously, for reasons explained at length in this chapter. On a theoretical level, the meaning of the concept of full cost reimbursement is thus unclear. A recent report on indirect costs by staff of the Department of Health and Human Services accurately states: "Under the cost reimbursement policy, the Federal Government agreed to pay for some portion of the direct and indirect, or overhead, costs of research. However, it has never been clear that full cost reimbursement has been the policy." Health and Human Services Working Group on the Costs of Research, "Management of Research Costs: Indirect Costs" (May 1992), p. 5.

3. HHS Working Group, *Management of Research Costs*, p. 23.

4. Ibid., p. 25.

5. James McCullough and Stephen Balut, *Cost Trends in the Defense Aircraft Industry*, IDA Publication D-764 (Alexandria, Va.: Institute for Defense Analysis, 1990).

6. See Robert K. Merton, "Priorities in Scientific Discovery: A Chapter in the Sociology of Science," *American Sociological Review*, vol. 22, no. 6 (December 1957), pp. 635–59; "The Matthew Effect in Science," *Science*, January 5, 1968, pp. 56–63; and Partha Dasgupta and Paul A. David, "Toward a New Economics of Science," *Research Policy*, vol. 23, no. 5 (September 1994), pp. 487–521.

7. See William Rogerson, "Profit Regulation of Defense Contractors and Prizes for Innovation," *Journal of Political Economy*, vol. 97, no. 6 (December 1989), pp. 1284–1305; and William Rogerson, "Economic Incentives and the Defense Procurement Process," *Journal of Economic Perspectives*, vol. 8, no. 4 (Fall 1994), pp. 65–90.

8. Kirk Monteverde and David J. Teece, "Supplier Switching Costs and Vertical Integration in the Automobile Industry," *Bell Journal of Economics*, vol. 13, no. 1 (Spring 1982), pp. 206–13.

9. Linda R. Cohen and Roger G. Noll, *The Technology Pork Barrel* (Brookings, 1991), pp. 37–52.

10. See Richard R. Nelson and Sidney G. Winter, *An Evolutionary Theory of Economic Change* (Harvard University Press, 1982).

11. For more information about the history of federal policies for contracting with universities for research projects, see the HHS Working Group, "Management of Research Costs," pp. 5–7.

12. Universities with a very low volume of sponsored research (under $3 million) can use a simpler process for accounting for indirect

costs. As discussed in chapter 1, all research universities receive substantially more than this amount in federal research grants.

13. Equipment is the major category that is excluded from the direct costs that are multiplied by the indirect cost rate to determine indirect cost recovery.

14. Why state universities follow this practice is a matter of some controversy. One plausible explanation is that some state governments require that public universities return indirect cost recovery to the state treasury (see HHS Working Group, *Management of Research Costs*, p. 26). As a result, the university has nothing to lose and possibly something to gain competitively by keeping indirect costs low and so reducing the bottom-line price that it charges the federal government for research. Another possible explanation is that state universities exclude depreciation of state-financed buildings and equipment because the federal government would force them to do so to maintain parity with the exclusion of federally financed facilities.

15. HHS Working Group, "Management of Research Costs," p. 18.

16. Rather than allowing universities to charge a fraction of faculty salaries to federal research grants, and then declaring this cost to be unallowable, federal agencies generally follow the essentially equivalent practice of requiring universities to practice "cost sharing" by paying all or most of the salaries of faculty who have research grants.

17. HHS Working Group, "Management of Research Costs," p. 18.

18. For a good discussion of the economic content and usefulness of accounting, see Joel S. Demski and Robert P. Magee, "A Perspective on Accounting for Defense Contracts," *Accounting Review*, vol. 67 (1992), pp. 732–40.

19. See William P. Rogerson, "Overhead Allocation and Incentives for Cost Minimization in Defense Procurement," *Accounting Review*, vol. 67 (1992), pp. 671–90.

20. For example, the Inspector General of HHS, among possible solutions to the problem of rising indirect cost rates, proposed that the federal government pay no more in indirect costs than the lowest rate offered to any entity and that even this rate be limited to expenditures for items that are incremental to federally sponsored research. Department of Health and Human Services, Office of the Inspector General, *Federal Funding to Colleges and Universities in Support of Research* (May 1991).

21. Presumably, the existence of these productive synergies is the reason that the activities are undertaken within a single organization in the first place.

22. Total federal obligations for science and engineering R&D were $144 million at the twenty-fourth leading institution, Arizona, in 1994. If, as estimated by the HHS Working Group ("Management of Research

Costs," p. 23), 30 percent of this revenue were indirect cost recovery, then Arizona collected slightly more than $100 million in direct costs. The leading institution was Johns Hopkins, with $613 million; however, a large part of this support was for a specialized research facility that is nearer a national laboratory than an academic research program. Washington, MIT, and Stanford rank below Johns Hopkins, with total R&D support of between $250 and $275 million, which translates to direct costs of under $200 million. See National Science Foundation, *Federal Science and Engineering Support to Universities, Colleges, and Nonprofit Institutions*, NSF 96–317 (Arlington, Va., 1996), p. 35.

23. In 1994 nearly $12 billion was granted to universities for research and development (not including facilities grants). Some of the latter funds are not for standard research projects but are allocations to research centers that have different accounting procedures. The government does not separate these allocations from the rest, but the vast majority of support is for ordinary project grants. For example, the National Institutes of Health and the National Science Foundation spent about $8 billion on R&D at universities in 1994, and almost all of the funds from these agencies are for standard project grants. If 30 percent of grant awards are for indirect cost (see note 22), the estimate of $3 billion for indirect cost recovery is not likely to be far off.

24. The administrative cost cap has two benchmarks: a lower amount (24 percent) that requires less justification, and a higher amount (26 percent) that requires more extensive justification. The thrust of our argument is that once one has set a cap roughly equal to average cost under the present system, there is no reason to audit actual expenditures for the purposes of determining whether the university actually spent more than the capped amount.

25. Association of American Universities, *Indirect Costs Associated with Federal Support of Research on University Campuses: Some Suggestions for Change* (Washington, December 1988). The report also recommended greater rationality in distinguishing direct and indirect costs, proposing that, generally speaking, more costs should be measured in a manner that allowed them to be part of direct costs. A similar but more limited proposal to set a single, unaudited rate for departmental research was proposed in U.S. General Accounting Office, Comptroller General, *Assuring Reasonableness of Rising Indirect Costs on NIH Research Grants—A Difficult Problem* (Washington: Government Accounting Office, March 16, 1984).

26. The HHS Working Group, in "Management of Research Costs," undertook a regression analysis of the components of indirect cost rates. It found that nearly all of the variance among universities could be explained by ownership (private or public), amount of research expenditures (a measure of quality), and region (to reflect differences in wages, utility prices, and construction costs).

Chapter 6

Soft Money, Hard Choices: Research Universities and University Hospitals

Linda R. Cohen

University hospitals provide a large share of the revenues of research universities. The statistics reported in chapter 2 show that sales at hospitals are the third largest source of revenues for all research universities and amount to about 16 percent of university revenues.[1] For those universities that report hospital sales as part of campus finances, the revenue share attributable to hospitals is more than 33 percent. In 1993–94, medical schools reported that nearly 50 percent of their revenues came from "medical services": practice plans and hospital payments.[2] In addition to underscoring the financial consequence of university hospitals, these statistics reveal an important attribute of research universities: the provision of health care is a significant activity.

Changes in health services in the United States are forcing nearly every academic medical center to reorganize. University hospitals are relatively expensive, charging 10 to 20 percent more than other hospitals for "equivalent" services.[3] To compete in the current market—where the specialist services that university hospitals provide are evidently oversupplied—these hospitals must become more cost efficient. Moreover, the growth of health maintenance organizations (HMOs) has undercut traditional sources of patient referrals to university hospitals, so most are seeking alternative ways to maintain their supply of patients. In addition, the threat of cuts in vital federal programs looms over medical schools and academic medical centers. Medicare provides more than $6 billion for graduate medical education through the Indirect Medical Education and Direct Medical Education programs (IME and DME) and pays about 25 percent of physician fees overall.[4] Medicaid gives more than $17 billion to the states for Disproportionate Share Hospital payments (DSH), most of which winds up at academic medical centers. The Health Care Financing Association, which administers these programs, has proposed reducing IME and DME payments and eliminating DSH altogether.[5]

Responses to the Changing Environment

University hospitals have pursued some combination of four strategies to deal with actual or anticipated financial crises: mergers, group practice affiliations, vertical integration, and divestiture. The first strategy attempts to directly address the issue of oversupply of tertiary care. Between 1994 and 1996 there were an extraordinary number of actual or planned mergers intended to improve efficiency, reduce redundancy, and place the hospitals in relatively better bargaining positions for contracts with managed care companies.[6]

The second thrust involves ensuring the provision of patients by affiliating with HMOs, primary care physicians, and community hospitals. These efforts generally resemble joint ventures but vary considerably. Nearly all university hospitals contract with managed care enterprises. Recently, managed care contracts have shifted from traditional fee-for-service arrangements to capitated payments, which involve receiving fixed payments in return for providing all hospital services (or a range of services agreed to ex ante) to HMO members. As a result, hospitals are assuming more risks and taking on the role of insurer. These arrangements are sometimes problematic. For example, concerns have arisen over the risks of capitated contracts without adequate control over HMO enrollments.[7] Also, some medical centers have found that their affiliations with other health providers are too tenuous to guarantee the referrals sought over an adequate period.[8]

The third strategy calls for vertical integration into primary care activities. Many university hospitals are affiliated with or own community hospitals, and a few own HMOs.[9] Perhaps the most aggressive practitioner of this strategy is the University of Pennsylvania, which created the University of Pennsylvania Health System in its 1993 strategic plan. John Inglehart reports that the enterprise "will include the university's major teaching hospital and its 750 attending physicians, its community-based network of doctors, three aligned community hospitals, outpatient facilities, nursing homes, rehabilitation centers, subacute care facilities and home health care."[10] The University of Pennsylvania is in the process of acquiring the primary care practices of 300 doctors and plans to enroll 600,000 people in its health care system.

The vertical integration strategy—and, to some degree, the other strategies outlined here—is also a response to other concerns about the academic medical establishment. A long-standing criticism of U.S. medical education is that far too many students are trained to be subspecialists, reflecting the patient load and research activities of medical school faculty. The University of Pennsylvania hopes to provide students with broader educational opportunities and also to integrate the specialized services of its central hospital more fully with the activities of other health care providers.[11]

Another opportunity provided by integration is to change the patient composition of the academic medical centers from its increasingly untenable mix. In a recent survey, community hospital chief executive officers (CEOs) characterized tertiary care (specifically, care at the University Hospital in Colorado) as "transplants, burns, trauma, severe diagnostic dilemmas, procedures that have faltered and need to be repeated or repaired, and, of course, uninsured patients, regardless of the disease process."[12] In 1991, academic medical centers reported nearly twice the rate of charity care and bad debt as a percent of net patient revenues as did nonteaching hospitals (9.6 percent versus 5.1 percent). The members of the Council on Teaching Hospitals accounted for nearly half of the country's charity care services (and about one-quarter of all hospital revenues).[13]

As a result, some universities are considering divestiture, with negotiated arrangements between the hospital corporation and medical school for medical education and clinical research activities. In response to difficulties in negotiating contractual relationships with private health care entities for patient referrals (that is, HMOs), pharmaceutical products, and other services, several states have established separate corporate entities with substantial independent negotiating authority for the hospitals associated with state university medical schools.[14] Separate corporate structures have been established at both public and private schools, though for some public universities the legality of the arrangements (where private corporate institutional structures have been attempted) is still unclear.[15] The most radical example of the divestiture strategy is at Tulane University, which sold 80 percent of its hospital to Columbia/HCA Healthcare, a for-profit corporation currently negotiating joint ownership, operations, or lease agreements with several other university hospitals.[16]

In this chapter I explore the implications of the changes under way at academic medical centers for the larger university structure. The next section presents an overview of the scope of the financial problems currently facing university hospitals and medical schools. The following section focuses on the proposed strategies that establish university-industry joint ventures for the provision of health care. Other public-private joint ventures in competitive industries have faced some peculiar problems. Specifically, the politics of competitive industries is such that in some cases government essentially constrains the enterprise's ability to succeed. I include a discussion of the reasons for these political difficulties and their potential applicability to the plans of academic medical centers.

The scale of the medical enterprise is far greater than for related commercial technology initiatives at universities. These include the efforts by universities to capitalize on intellectual property rights and enter into joint ventures with high-tech firms, and the more established activities of engineering research centers (discussed in chapter 7). Nevertheless, the outcomes of other public-private joint ventures are relevant to the likely results of the university hospital reorganizations. Similarly, the problems that have surfaced in the course of hospital reorganizations so far may have broader implications for other university-industry collaborations.

Competition and Financial Losses

Critics of university hospital reorganizations have focused on short-term implications for medical education and medical research. Their fears are essentially twofold: subsidies for the medical schools will decline, if not disappear, and efforts to generate profits will further damage medical school research and education.[17]

Medical school financing has changed dramatically over the past twenty years. As with universities overall, grants and contracts are a declining share of revenues (from 54 percent in 1970–71 to under 25 percent in 1991–92). Grants and contracts had real growth of nearly 100 percent over this period. However, the health education enterprise grew in real dollars by more than 300 percent (see table 6-1). Alternatively, medical service plans increased from under 7 percent to 32 percent during the same period.[18] Observers universally claim that with the post–World War II increase in federal biomedical research support, the focus of medical schools shifted from education to research. Some add that medical schools have increasingly focused on the more lucrative medical specialties, but usually not at the expense of research.[19] To some degree, the impact of the shift in financing over the past twenty years has been blunted by cross-subsidies from hospital and clinical revenues into research and education.

For 1993–94, medical schools reported that 33 percent of their revenues were derived from practice plans and 13 percent from hospital programs.[20] The former category consists of fees paid to faculty physicians by patients. The typical arrangement at medical schools is that all clinical fees are considered payments to (or initially collected by) the university, which then deducts an average of 16 percent for academic programs, including a "dean's tax" (5 percent) and department support (10 percent). Of the remainder, 42 percent recirculates into physician compensation, 1 per-

Table 6-1. Revenues of U.S. Medical Schools

Millions of 1996 dollars

Year	Total federal government $	Percent	State and local government $	Percent	Tuition and fees $	Percent	Medical services $	Percent	Other $	Percent	Total $	Percent
1960–61	904	41	380	17	144	6	144	6	668	30	2,239	100
1965–66	2,200	53	639	15	193	5	230	6	884	21	4,146	100
1970–71	2,882	45	1,225	19	239	4	793	12	1,358	21	6,497	100
1975–76	3,413	36	2,192	24	423	5	1,652	18	1,614	18	9,196	100
1980–81	3,754	31	2,798	23	648	5	3,219	27	1,648	14	12,067	100
1985–86	3,901	25	3,185	20	888	6	5,336	34	2,382	15	15,692	100
1986–87	4,108	24	3,217	19	922	5	6,526	38	2,571	15	17,344	100
1987–88	4,486	23	3,307	18	964	5	7,246	38	2,828	15	18,832	100
1988–89	4,790	23	3,420	16	986	5	9,037	42	3,291	15	21,523	100
1989–90	5,256	23	3,515	15	1,004	4	9,836	42	355	15	23,166	100
1990–91	5,400	22	3,484	14	1,032	4	11,083	45	3,734	15	24,733	100
1991–92	5,746	22	3,307	13	1,084	4	12,261	47	3,904	15	26,302	100
1992–93	6,014	21	3,278	12	1,157	4	13,237	47	4,198	15	27,885	100
1993–94	6,288	21	3,282	11	1,221	4	14,634	49	4,311	14	29,736	100

Source: *AAMC Data Book, 1994* (Washington: American Association of Medical Colleges, 1994), table D3; Janice L. Ganem, Robert L. Beran, and Jack K. Krakower, "Review of US Medical School Finances, 1993–1994," *Journal of the American Medical Association*, September 6, 1995, table 4.

cent goes to house staff and clinical fellow support, and 39 percent to "other expenses."

Jones and Sanderson have analyzed the distribution of practice plan revenues and conclude that about 28 percent goes toward academic programs and the remainder toward supporting the clinical enterprise.[21] They conclude further that this 28 percent can be divided into support for undergraduate education (8 percent), research (10 percent), graduate medical education (7 percent), and other activities (3 percent). The analysis is based on the notion that the value of time spent by physician-professors on all activities is identical, so that if a disproportionate share of their income is derived from clinical work, it subsidizes the time spent teaching and doing research.[22]

For many medical school professors, the research subsidy is more direct. A fairly standard arrangement is that faculty are required to cover their salary through clinical fees, grants, contracts, and explicit teaching arrangements. If clinical income is sufficient, they are not required to charge own-salary time on grants. However, if clinical income falls and faculty want to spend time on research (which the hospital of the future is not expected to support), they would have to charge research time to grants. Federal expenditures for biomedical research grants still enjoy a positive real rate of growth; however, this growth is insufficient to absorb a much larger fraction of faculty salaries and in any case is projected to turn negative before the year 2000 (see chapter 4).

The projected drop in patient practice revenues is therefore claimed to hurt medical schools on two counts: the direct subsidy (dean's tax, etc.) will decline, and the indirect subsidy (physician time) will also.[23] The usual presumption is that physician-professors, to maintain income levels, will spend more time in clinical practice. A study of the HMO enrollment necessary if University of Michigan professors are to maintain the level of professional specialty revenue to which they have become accustomed concluded that managed care enrollees would have to number in the millions. In fact, for most departments, at least 10 percent of Michigan's population would need to subscribe.[24] The expected outcome is that some specialists must go, incomes will drop, the remaining doctors will see more patients, and both research and education will suffer.[25]

Increased competition introduces other changes beyond the observed reduction in clinical faculty compensation. Indeed, compensation for many physicians, not just clinical faculty, is declining. It is reasonable to expect that compensation of clinical faculty may fall even more sharply—in particular, by the extent to which it subsidizes other medical school activities that are largely public goods. Evidence from deregulated industries suggests that increased competition leads to a reduction in support for research that has substantial public goods attributes. For example, anticipating rate deregulation, California utilities withdrew from the Electric Power Research Institute, the consortium of private electric utilities that sponsors generic research.[26] The cutbacks at some famous industrial research laboratories, most prominently Bell Labs and then Bellcore, are similarly credited at least in part to increased competition.

Only a fraction of research support can be characterized as having predominantly public goods characteristics; however, this type of research includes activities traditionally associated with universities—nonproprietary, published results. Indeed, to the extent that research results can lead to private profits (including commercialization of scientific ideas), expenditures may increase with competition: in general, increased competition is associated with increases in research and development activities in an industry and more rapid rates of growth in productivity.[27] However, among the features that distinguish industrial research in competitive industries from university research (at least in degree) are industrial projects that tend to be relatively short term, potential commercial applications clearly identified at the outset of the project, and scientists who specifically account for their time on various projects. It is likely that the R&D pursued by for-profit or competing firms in the medical services industry will follow the industrial R&D model in these respects, rather than the university model.

Another feature of a competitive environment is that it introduces a large element of risk to hospital revenues. One advantage to creating a separate corporate body that assumes ownership of a hospital (even if it is a fully-owned subsidiary of the university, as in the case of the University of Chicago) is that it limits the university's liability. Given the scale of the hospital activities relative to the university total, the risks they present in the context of a competitive industry are significant. Many university practices—in particular, the long-term or permanent employment contracts for senior faculty—mesh poorly with uncertain revenues.

In sum, the fears universities have about the reduction in subsidies from university hospitals are well founded. To the extent that hospitals must operate in a competitive environment, their ability to compensate faculty-physicians in a manner that cross-subsidizes medical school activities is reduced. Furthermore, the nature of the research sponsored by hospitals and the contractual relationship between the hospital and clinical faculty are likely to change in character and diverge even further from the university's traditional activities.

Problems are escalating at many academic medical centers. Layoffs (or, more commonly, rumors of layoffs) of nontenured faculty members and restrictions on soft-money appointments are taking place. Plans to limit tenure for new hires are being considered.[28] Many schools are tightening compensation plans (the arrangements under which physician practice income is allocated between the school and its physicians). In an effort to streamline operations, improve accountability, and respond to HMOs, which prefer to contract with a single entity, schools are replacing individual practices and department-based clinical groups with schoolwide control of clinical practices.[29]

The differences between the organizational imperatives of medical schools and university hospitals have given rise to increasing tension between the two. At a conference in 1995, Robert Michels, dean of the Cornell University Medical School, noted: "Tensions between medical schools and hospitals are infamous. Academia's collegial approach to decisionmaking and governance is different from the health care industry's hierarchical approach. Such tensions can be healthy, and they may be inevitable: but they have increased as the business problems of hospitals have grown and the rate of change in the goals of academic programs has become more rapid."[30] At the same conference, Robert Petersdorf and Kathleen Turner (president and vice president, respectively, of the Association of American Medical Colleges) observed:

> Medical schools, like other institutions, tend to respond to change slowly, purportedly so that the traditions of scholarship are protected, whereas a hospital must be able to adapt rapidly to a fluctuating marketplace. The management practices of the hospital and the medical school intersect in the faculty practice plan, which constitutes a progressively greater financial and operational piece of the AMC. Operationally, the practice plan needs to be managed more like the hospital than like the medical school, which often makes it a source of tension between the two. When clinical faculty work as employees, partners, or part owners of a practice plan, they are often neither faculty nor hospital staff. As a progressively greater portion of their income becomes dependent on the generation of private practice, the faculty's existence becomes more schizophrenic.[31]

The issues reviewed here suggest that fundamental changes are occurring at academic medical centers, regardless of the reorganizations currently under consideration. In the recent past, subsidies for research and education were substantial; these will decline. Retrenchment (particularly in some medical specialties) is inevitable. Financial insecurity and shifts in the types of research program that hospitals are likely to retain imply that the structure of academic medical centers will diverge from other parts of universities. Moreover, activities associated with education, basic science, medical research, and provision of medical care will likely become more distinct. Indeed, one of the proposals receiving serious attention at some schools is the idea of segregating academic medical centers into several distinct operations:

moving basic science departments into the university; establishing an independent professional medical school emphasizing undergraduate (pre-M.D.) medical education; creating a separate medical research institute (not necessarily affiliated with the university); and organizing university hospitals under a separate corporate structure, possibly for profit.[32] (This option is considered further in a later section of this chapter.)

Competition and Financial Profits

The prospect of excess profits at university hospitals is not currently troubling for many university presidents or hospital administrators. However, the juxtaposition of profits with other public-private collaborations has been accompanied by some significant problems. It is therefore worth remembering the adage about being careful what one wishes for.

Since World War II, research universities have consistently argued that their science activities contribute to technological development and economic growth.[33] Moreover, the traditional view of the university contribution distinguishes it from private firms along two key dimensions. University research tends to be basic or fundamental, providing an input for technological development by firms or individuals, and it does so without discrimination or fee. In addition, the global economic contribution of university research may be difficult to measure (notwithstanding the recent attempts to do so), particularly at or close to the time that university investments are undertaken.

Of course, this view of the university is both idealized and incomplete. Yet it is at the heart of the social contract between universities and the government, justifying the substantial subsidies provided to universities by government and philanthropists and the relative lack of strings attached to these funds.[34] The internal organization of universities supports and furthers the social contract. Basing promotion on peer-reviewed publication, encouraging open collegial collaborations, and emphasizing teaching and training provide mechanisms for external evaluations of university research in the absence of direct market tests and also promote the diffusion of research results.

The view of universities as suppliers of free knowledge has never characterized U.S. research universities accurately. Indeed, since at least the beginning of the twentieth century, some universities have profited directly from royalties from patented university research and other technology transfer activities.[35] The ability of universities to patent (that is, privatize) results from federally sponsored research was codified in the Bayh-Dole Act of 1980 and extended in subsequent legislation. Today royalty revenues are an important source of income at some universities. In addition, other recent federal initiatives have promoted joint university-industry technology ventures. However, as discussed in chapter 7, these initiatives have been controversial.

Complaints tend to hark back to the social contract, specifically claiming that the university has privatized research that belongs to all. An early example is the case of the process to synthesize vitamin D, which was discovered by scientists at the University of Wisconsin and patented by the Wisconsin Alumni Research Fund (WARF) for the financial benefit of research at the university. The patent was not contested, but WARF (at the behest of the scientists) licensed the process only to butter producers and excluded all margarine producers. This created an uproar, and, following an antitrust challenge, WARF reversed its policy.

Notwithstanding recent legislation, the question remains: to what extent will universities be allowed to capitalize on their research activities? The experience at both universities and other public-private joint ventures suggests that substantial problems are likely to arise when the "public" (in this case, university) activity ventures into competitive industries. This experience in turn implies that the prospects for joint ventures between industry and university hospitals will grow increasingly problematic.

The federal government has undertaken a series of policy initiatives to encourage joint research ventures that have some similarities to the changes under way at university hospitals.[36] These programs have generated a set of problems that may be relevant to the university hospital proposals.

The new programs allow government laboratories to help private firms develop new technology (through subsidy or joint research) in which a firm owns property rights that it expects to commercialize. As with any new technology, the projects have the potential of transferring wealth: from consumers to a monopoly producer (that is, a patent-holder); from firms whose products become obsolete to those that successfully commercialize technology with the government's help; and from upstream firms to downstream firms, or vice versa. Given the norm that the public sector's largesse belongs to all, many of the programs have been hailed as "unfair" and in a variety of ways have had their wings clipped.

One example is the case of the Cooperative Research and Development Agreements (CRADAs) at the National Institutes of Health (NIH). NIH aided in the development of several successful drugs, including AZT (azidothymidine, or zidovudine) and Taxol (paclitaxel), which became highly profitable to pharmaceutical companies. In the case of AZT, the price initially charged to consumers was deemed outrageous. A dispute over Taxol arose over which pharmaceutical company would win the right to develop the drug jointly with NIH. Though NIH's actions were legal (and were upheld in court), Congress held contentious hearings in response to complaints. In the early 1990s, it required that any contracts NIH entered into with companies for collaborative research contain a highly unpopular "fair price clause," specifying that any resulting products would be sold at a fair price.

CRADA pricing policies are still evolving. Currently, pharmaceutical companies are required to price CRADA products in a manner that reflects the public contribution to the invention. The accounting procedures for establishing the validity of pricing policies are unclear. However, they are believed to have had a chilling effect on NIH's ability to enter into cooperative joint development projects with private firms.[37]

Another problem surfaced at Sematech, a consortium of semiconductor manufacturers formed in 1987 for joint technology development. Sematech received an allocation from the Defense Advanced Research Projects Agency amounting to about half of its operating budget. The complaints about Sematech came from two sources. One was semiconductor manufacturers that were not members of Sematech but that nevertheless argued for access to any new technology by virtue of the government subsidy. The other source of complaints was semiconductor equipment manufacturers, who signed contracts with Sematech, receiving a subsidy for developing new equipment. In return, these manufacturers agreed that all new machines developed under the contract would be sold exclusively to Sematech members for the first three years that they were produced. The semiconductor equipment manufacturers claimed (after the fact) that Sematech constituted a downstream cartel established (unfairly) by government. After being forced to release technology to nonmember firms and to loosen agreements with equipment manufacturers, members of Sematech started dropping out of the consortium. In 1995, Sematech declared victory and renounced its government subsidy.

Several lessons can be drawn from these stories. First, exclusive arrangements can be successfully challenged. The charge that public resources should not be used to help some businesses while hurting others has compelling political appeal. In addition, the ability of the public sector to modify arrangements is not constrained by the initial legality of these arrangements or their success in accomplishing their original goals (for example, inventing useful new technology and helping business). Indeed, political problems typically arise only when projects are economically successful. Finally, the problems summarized here will most likely arise in competitive industries.[38]

Government has a long if not altogether successful history of involvement in subsidizing technical development and other operations in regulated industries, where these problems are less likely to surface.[39] The AZT problem, for example, would not have arisen in an industry in which firms are subject to price regulation. Moreover, regulated firms are unlikely to complain about one another's activities because they do not compete. Indeed, such firms have no reason to restrict research results from each other, as evidenced by the research consortia that successfully operated among electric utilities.[40]

These issues are not foreign to the health care industry. Paul Starr describes numerous cases of difficulties encountered by public health organizations when their activities crossed the boundary between the public and private sectors. For example, in the late nineteenth century, the New York City Health Department manufactured diphtheria antitoxin for emergencies and sold off excess serum. As Starr notes: "In April 1902, over a thousand physicians and druggists signed a petition urging the mayor to root out this continued 'commercialism' in the health department. Later that year the department announced it would cease all outside sale of antitoxin," losing the income that had paid the salaries of departmental employees.[41]

Some of the new arrangements for university hospitals bear enough similarities to the cases described above to raise concerns. The basic similarity is that university hospitals operate in an increasingly competitive health market, and one competing more and more against other hospitals, HMOs, and private practices. If the university succeeds in this market, its competitors lose. Even if competition is not a zero-sum game, it can appear that way to an unsuccessful firm. If the competitors allege that the university hospital's advantage is due to public investment, the hospital will have at the very least a public relations problem. At worst, the public entities that provide public support for the university (state legislatures and Congress) may withdraw their support.

For example, by virtue of its research and educational facilities, a university hospital may provide some unique or particularly good tertiary care services.[42] If these facilities are to be a selling point for a university HMO, its members must have preferential access. If the hospital were private, competing HMOs would be stuck with market forces. But if the hospital is quasi-public, competitors have an alternative. They can complain to politicians about the abusive use of tax dollars by the university— an institution that obtained those dollars with the promise of providing public goods for all of society—that gives an unfair advantage to the university HMO.

Joint ventures with affiliated HMOs have similar potential problems. If the university chooses to affiliate with a single HMO, the situation is analogous to the CRADA cases discussed previously, in which a government lab collaborates with a single firm or exclusive group of firms. An alternative option (which would appear to obviate unfair access claims) is for the university hospital to offer contracts to any HMO in its region. However, the terms of the contracts call for careful scrutiny. Quantity discounts, for example, may discriminate against small organizations. That such discounts are economically justified is not necessarily a defense. For example, any U.S. semiconductor manufacturing firm could have joined Sematech. That some chose not to join did not detract from their ability to induce the federal government to prevent the consortium from denying them access to its products.

The case of University Hospital in Denver, Colorado, suggests that these concerns are of more than theoretical interest. The University of Colorado School of Medicine faculty are organized in a physician group called UPI, which practices at University Hospital (now a distinct corporation from the university). The chief competitor of UPI is Health One, an entity formed by other major hospitals in the Denver area, including Swedish Hospital. The School of Medicine (SOM) recently initiated a graduate medical education program at Swedish that, according to its dean, presented the school "with a serious conflict. On the one hand, the SOM is a state entity and has a responsibility to all of its alumni and clinical faculty. On the other hand, UPI . . . is the competitor of Health One, and as a practice group, it is viscerally opposed to providing [graduate medical education] to the opposition, putting the dean, who is also president of the practice plan in an interesting, albeit schizoid, position."[43] The dean, in common with others, concluded that the ability of the University Hospital (and the SOM physician practice group) to obtain a competitive advantage from its close relationship with the medical school is limited.[44]

Soft Money, Hard Choices

Over the past twenty-five years, research universities became heavily involved in the provision of health services. In the 1980s, health care was perceived as an easy source of soft money for medical schools and a logical extension of their education and research missions. Today, the softness of the money has become only too evident, and universities are scrambling for ways to maintain the viability of their academic medical centers.

Competition in the health care industry brings more concerns than simply those that focus on the bottom line. The incentives for and interactions among health care providers are fundamentally changing. The increasingly competitive nature of the industry suggests that universities will face political as well as economic difficulties in participating in the market on a large scale. There is substantial evidence (admittedly aggravating) that the political sector is inclined to meddle in those public sector enterprises that compete successfully with private sector constituents. These problems are likely to be most acute at public universities, but private universities also profess the public service goals of the public sector and get substantial public support. They too are vulnerable.

Most universities have concluded that to continue to operate hospitals, they must offer "integrated health services," not just the tertiary care traditionally provided by their hospitals. As a result, they are expanding the range of health services that they offer, either by themselves or through affiliations or joint ventures with other entities. The long-term success of these plans is problematic.

Stuart Bondurant, former dean of the medical school at the University of North Carolina, has challenged the integrated academic medical center model. He argues that "the research that is now performed is, in general, more removed from the bedside than it used to be. . . . Much of the current biomedical research might be better performed in other kinds of institutions." Furthermore, he notes, "medicine is unique among the professions in the extent to which practice is an essential part of teaching. This association may, however, be due for reexamination."[45]

Little systematic research has addressed whether there are complementaries between the variety of activities now undertaken by academic medical centers (undergraduate and graduate education, basic science, clinical research, and clinical services).[46] The extent of the complementarities and the nature of the synergies are clearly key issues. If, as is argued here, the quasi-public status of universities constrains their ability to participate effectively in a competitive market, and if clinical research, clinical care, and other educational and research activities are becoming segregated at academic medical centers, then it is difficult to justify the university's continuing role as a major provider of health care.

Endnotes

1. This is an underestimate of health services revenues, as the statistics in chapter 2 include only universities that report hospital sales as part of the campus revenues in their response to the Department of Education Integrated Postsecondary Education Data System survey. Only half of the research universities with medical schools (thirty-six out of the seventy Carnegie Schools that the AAHC *Membership Directory* lists as having a medical school) report sales from hospitals on this survey, although nearly all own at least one hospital and are affiliated with four or more (a list of affiliations is included in AAHC *Membership Directory* [Washington: Association of Academic Health Centers, 1994]). In addition, some schools report practice plan revenues under the "Sales of Educational Activities" category.

2. Janice L. Ganem, Robert L. Beran, and Jack K. Krakower, "Review of U.S. Medical School Finances, 1993–1994," *Journal of the American Medical Association,* vol. 274, no. 9 (1995), pp. 723–30.

3. Because the services offered by academic hospitals differ from those of community hospitals, the cost-comparison is tricky. Estimates in 1991 suggest that the incremental costs associated with medical education and research were on the order of $9 billion. Gerard Anderson, Earl Steinberg, and Robert Heyssel, "The Pivotal Role of the Academic Health Center," *Health Affairs,* vol. 13, no. 3 (Summer 1994), p. 150. See also John K. Inglehart, "The American Health Care System—Teaching Hospitals," *New England Journal of Medicine,* vol. 329, no. 14 (September 30, 1993), pp. 1052–56; Gerard F. Anderson and others, *Providing Hospital Services: The Changing Financial Environment* (Johns Hopkins University Press, 1989). Some estimates place the cost differential as high as 30 percent. Eli Ginzberg, "Perspectives," in Ginzberg, ed., *Urban Medical Centers: Balancing Academic and Patient Care Functions* (Boulder, Colo.: Westview Press, 1996), p. 86.

4. Congressional Budget Office, *Medicare and Graduate Medical Education* (September 1995), p. ix.

5. Bruce C. Vladeck, "Academic Health Centers: Financing and Future Options," in David E. Rogers and Eli Ginzberg, eds., *The Metro-*

politan Academic Medical Center: Its Role in an Era of Tight Money and Changing Expectations (Boulder, Colo.: Westview Press, 1995), p. 75–76.

6. In 1996 merger discussions and plans were under way at Hahnemann and the Medical College of Pennsylvania, Brigham and Women's Hospital and Massachusetts General Hospital, SUNY Health Science Center at Brooklyn and King's County, Indiana University and Methodist Hospital, UC San Francisco and Stanford, Boston City Hospital and Boston University Medical School, and New York Hospital and Presbyterian Hospital. The affiliation strategies tend toward complexity. John K. Inglehart, "Academic Medical Centers Enter the Market: The Case of Philadelphia," *New England Journal of Medicine,* vol. 333, no. 15 (1995a), pp. 1019–1023; David Firestone, "Brooklyn Hospitals on a Shared Mission: SUNY and Kings County, Wary Neighbors for Years, Seek to Unite," *New York Times,* April 11, 1994, p. B3; Eliot Marshall, "UCSF, Stanford Hospitals to Merge," *Science,* vol. 272 (May 17, 1996), p. 944; Elizabeth Rosenthal, "2 More Hospitals Decide to Merge in New York City," *New York Times,* July 25, 1996, p. A1. For further discussion and examples, see Goldie Blumenstyk, "Reform at Medical Centers: Universities Make Some Dramatic Changes to Protect Their Hospitals and Clinics," *Chronicle of Higher Education,* July 13, 1994, pp. A25–A26; Amy Goldstein, "GW Hospital Seeks Buyer, Plans Layoffs," *Washington Post,* July 14, 1995, p. A1; and Ron Winslow, "Getting Down to Business at Duke's Medical School," *Wall Street Journal,* August 29, 1995, p. B1.

7. James A. Block, "Getting to Health Reform: Faulty Maps, Poor Directions," in David E. Rogers and Eli Ginzberg, eds., *The Metropolitan Academic Medical Center: Its Role in an Era of Tight Money and Changing Expectations* (Boulder, Colo.: Westview Press, 1995), p. 48.

8. Ginzberg, "Perspectives," p. 88. See also Leo Henikoff, "Competition: A View of the Midwest," pp. 35–44, in Ginzberg, *Urban Medical Centers.*

9. For a commentary on this trend, see Stephen Abrahamson, "When Is a School Not a School?" *Academic Medicine,* vol. 71, no. 1 (January 1996), pp. 13–14.

10. Inglehart, "Academic Medical Centers Enter the Market," p. 1022.

11. William N. Kelley, "Gathering Momentum for the Next Century: Our Long-Range Strategic Plan," in Eli Ginzberg, ed., *Urban Medical Centers: Balancing Academic and Patient Care Functions* (Boulder, Colo.: Westview Press, 1996), pp. 61–66.

12. Richard D. Krugman, "Positioning an Academic Medical School for Survival: How Many Moving Targets Must We Hit to Make It?" in Eli Ginzberg, ed., *Urban Medical Centers: Balancing Academic and Patient Care Functions* (Boulder, Colo.: Westview Press, 1996), p. 53, note 3.

13. American Association of Medical Colleges, *AAMC Data Book* (Washington: 1994), table G-11.

14. Peter Schmidt, "Medical Autonomy: States Loosen Their Control over the Management of University Hospitals," *Chronicle of Higher Education,* February 16, 1996, pp. A27–A28. See also Krugman, "Positioning an Academic Medical School for Survival."

15. See, for example, Krugman, "Positioning an Academic Medical School for Survival," p. 46.

16. Schmidt, "Medical Autonomy," p. A28. In the early 1980s, Creighton University and the University of Louisville sold their university hospitals to for-profit corporations. Harvard University has always been structurally independent of its affiliated teaching hospitals, although owing to its large, coveted, independent endowment and other unique features, the Massachusetts General Hospital arrangement is generally rejected as a model for other schools.

17. A distinguished critic is Dr. Arnold S. Relman, former editor of the *New England Journal of Medicine,* who criticizes the joint ventures with for-profit corporations as "a Faustian bargain. . . . They are not in business to provide support for academic institutions. They are in business to make money." Alternatively, Chancellor LaRosa, of Tulane University, observes that "academic medical centers have made a substantial amount of money from clinical income for many, many years." Other defenders point out that with no money, the centers will certainly have no mission. Schmidt, "Medical Autonomy," p. A28.

18. American Association of Medical Colleges, *AAMC Data Book,* table D-2.

19. See, for example, Abrahamson, "When Is a School Not a School?"

20. Robert F. Jones and Susan C. Sanderson, "Clinical Revenues Used to Support the Academic Mission of Medical Schools, 1992–93," *Academic Medicine,* vol. 71, no. 3 (March 1996), pp. 300–307.

21. Jones and Sanderson, "Clinical Revenues Used to Support the Academic Mission."

22. Jones and Sanderson, "Clinical Revenues Used to Support the Academic Mission." The authors report that the "hospital support" category, some 13 percent of medical school revenues, is calculated so differently at different institutions that it was not possible to break it down in a fashion similar to that done for patient practice revenues. This category includes "all funding the medical school receives for providing services to hospitals and clinics. It also includes house staff stipends and salaries of faculty and support staff, as well as operating support for discrete activities that materially support medical school education, research, and patient care." Janice L. Ganem, Jack K. Krakower, and Robert L. Beran, "Review of U.S. Medical School Finances, 1992–1993," *Journal of the American Medical Association,* vol. 272, no. 9 (September 7, 1994), p. 705. Some unknown fraction of this category thus also represents a

subsidy to the "public good" activities of the medical school, and another represents salary increments for faculty.

23. As of 1993–94, patient practice revenues were still posting real increases. Ganem, Beran, and Krakower, "Review of U.S. Medical School Finances, 1993–1994."

24. John E. Billi and others, "Potential Effects of Managed Care of Specialty Practice at a University Medical Center," *New England Journal of Medicine,* October 12, 1995, pp. 979–83.

25. A standard economic argument actually would conclude the reverse: as clinical practice wages decline, faculty would shift activities into the less lucrative (but not by as much) research sphere, and thus spend *more* time engaged in research. When I proposed this theory to medical school deans and other people associated with academic medical centers, I was met with what might politely be called skepticism.

26. Linda R. Cohen, "When Can Government Subsidize Research Joint Ventures? Politics, Economics, and Limits to Technology Policy," American Economic Association, *Papers and Proceedings,* vol. 84, no. 2 (1994), pp. 159–63.

27. See Wesley M. Cohen and Richard C. Levin, "Empirical Studies of Innovation and Market Structure," in Richard Schmalensee and Robert D. Willig, eds., *The Handbook of Industrial Organization,* vol. 2 (New York: North Holland, 1989), pp. 1059–1107; Martin Neil Bailey and Hans Gersbach, "Efficiency in Manufacturing and the Need for Global Competition," *Brookings Papers on Economic Activity: Microeconomics* (1995), pp. 307–47.

28. Denise K. Magner, "Medical Schools Consider Limiting Tenure, Cutting Salaries," *Chronicle of Higher Education,* February 16, 1996, p. A18.

29. James E. Lewis, "Improving Productivity: The Ongoing Experience of an Academic Department of Medicine," *Academic Medicine,* vol. 71, no. 4 (1996), pp. 317–23; John K. Inglehart, "Rapid Changes for Academic Medical Centers, Part One," *New England Journal of Medicine,* vol. 332, no. 6 (1995b), pp. 1391–95; Inglehart, "Rapid Changes for Academic Medical Centers, Part Two," *New England Journal of Medicine,* vol. 332, no. 6 (February 9, 1995), pp. 407–11.

30. Robert Michels, "Tensions in the Metropolitan Academic Medical Center," in David E. Rogers and Eli Ginzberg, eds., *The Metropolitan Academic Medical Center: Its Role in an Era of Tight Money and Changing Expectations* (Boulder, Colo.: Westview Press, 1995), p. 71.

31. Robert G. Petersdorf and Kathleen S. Turner, "Are Academic Medical Centers in Trouble?" in David E. Rogers and Eli Ginzberg, eds., *The Metropolitan Academic Medical Center: Its Role in an Era of Tight Money and Changing Expectations* (Boulder, Colo.: Westview Press, 1995), p. 34.

32. See, for example, Stuart Bondurant, "Reinventing Education in Medical Schools," in Eli Ginzberg, ed., *Urban Medical Centers: Balancing*

Academic and Patient Care Functions (Boulder, Colo.: Westview Press, 1996), pp. 55–59.

33. For more details on the "social contract" and discussion of policies that raise concerns related to those discussed here, see Harvey Brooks, "Research Universities and the Social Contract for Science," in Lewis M. Branscomb, ed., *Empowering Technology: Implementing a U.S. Strategy* (MIT Press, 1993), pp. 202–234. Extensive literature discusses the importance of scientific diffusion for growth. See, for example, Paul David, David Mowery, and Edward Steinmuller, "Analyzing the Economic Payoffs from Basic Research," *Economics of Innovation and New Technologies*, vol. 2, no. 4 (1992), pp. 73–90; Adam B. Jaffe, "Real Effects of Academic Research," *American Economic Review*, vol. 79, no. 5 (December 1989), pp. 957–70; Edwin Mansfield, "Academic Research and Industrial Innovation," *Research Policy*, vol. 20, no. 1 (1991), pp. 1–12; Nathan Rosenberg, *Inside the Black Box: Technology and Economics* (Cambridge University Press, 1982); Bruce L. R. Smith and Claude Barfield, eds., *Technology, R&D and the Economy* (Brookings and the American Enterprise Institute, 1996).

34. Richard R. Nelson, "The Simple Economics of Basic Scientific Research," *Journal of Political Economy* (1959), pp. 297–306; Kenneth Arrow, "Economic Welfare and the Allocation of Resources for Invention," in Kenneth Arrow, ed., *Essays in the Theory of Risk-Bearing* (North Holland, 1970), pp. 144–64.

35. See Gary W. Matkin, *Technology Transfer and the American Research University* (New York: American Council on Education, 1990).

36. Linda R. Cohen and Roger G. Noll, "Privatizing Public Research: The New Competitiveness Strategy," in Ralph Landau, Timothy Taylor, and Gavin Wright, eds., *The Mosaic of Economic Growth* (Stanford University Press, 1996), pp. 305–33; Brooks, "Research Universities and the Social Contract for Science."

37. Linda R. Cohen and Roger G. Noll, "Feasibility of Effective Public-Private R&D Collaboration: The Case of Cooperative R&D Agreements," *International Journal of the Economics of Business*, vol. 2, no. 2 (1995), pp. 223–40.

38. See Sematech, "Sematech—1991 Update," Technology Transfer Doc. 9101044A-GEN (Austin, Texas, 1991); Brink Lindsey, "Dram Scam," *Reason*, vol. 22, no. 9 (February 1992), pp. 40–48; U.S. Congress, *Foreign Acquisition of Semi-Gas Systems*, Hearings before the Subcommittee on Science, Technology and Space of the Senate Committee on Commerce, Science and Transportation, 101 Cong. 2 sess. (Government Printing Office, October 10, 1990). For a more detailed discussion of the Sematech experience, see Linda R. Cohen and Roger G. Noll, "Research and Development," in Henry J. Aaron and Charles L. Schultze, eds., *Setting Domestic Priorities: What Can Government Do?* (Brookings, 1992), pp. 223–65.

39. Linda R. Cohen and Roger G. Noll, *The Technology Pork Barrel* (Brookings, 1991).

40. Cohen, "When Can Government Subsidize Research Joint Ventures?"

41. Paul Starr, *The Social Transformation of American Medicine* (Basic Books, 1982), p. 187.

42. Another situation relevant to academic medical centers, although not directly related to hospitals, is if, through a biotech joint venture, a particularly profitable product is developed. The possibility then exists for an AZT-type response.

43. Krugman, "Positioning an Academic Medical School for Survival," p. 53, note 5.

44. See also Bondurant, "Reinventing Education in Medical Schools."

45. Bondurant, "Reinventing Education in Medical Schools," p. 56.

46. See Anderson, Steinberg, and Heyssel, "The Pivotal Role of the Academic Health Center."

Chapter 7

Industry and the Academy: Uneasy Partners in the Cause of Technological Advance

Wesley M. Cohen, Richard Florida,
Lucien Randazzese, and John Walsh

The relationship between academic research and industrial R&D has come under intense scrutiny in the past
fifteen years. Academic research is perceived to be both
too distant from the needs of most industries and, for those few
industries where its relevance is apparent, too close to industry.
Reflecting the predominant sentiment that academic research is
too distant from industry, policymakers, motivated by government spending constraints and stiffening international economic
competition, have called on universities to advance commercial
technology more effectively by making their science and engineering research more relevant to industry's needs. Even the
National Science Foundation has embraced this mission with creation of the Science and Technology Centers and other programs
that tie support to industrial participation. At the same time,
controversy has been sparked by concerns that academic research
has grown too close to industry in areas such as biotechnology.
Critics fear that deepening commercial ties in such areas may be
undermining academe's commitment to both basic research as

The authors thank Richard Nelson, a collaborator on a related project, for helpful discussions, and David Hounshell for comments.

171

well as the academic norm of free disclosure—a norm that contributes to research quality and to the cumulative advance of science and engineering more generally.[1]

Stimulated by these controversies, in this chapter we examine new survey evidence along with other recent findings to assess the impact of university research on industrial R&D. We also look at the effect of ties with industry on the conduct of academic research in science and engineering. We then consider possible implications of this evidence for the cause of technological advance itself.

This chapter draws heavily on two survey research projects in which the authors have been involved. The first examines university-industry R&D centers in the United States.[2] The second considers the impact of university R&D on industrial R&D for the U.S. manufacturing sector, as well as a broad range of other issues bearing on the nature and determinants of industrial R&D.[3]

The Effect of University R&D on Industry

This section briefly reviews recent findings on the effects of university research in science and engineering on industrial R&D and then reports selected findings from the 1994 Carnegie Mellon Survey on Industrial R&D in the U.S. manufacturing sector. Most of the findings from both the literature and the recent surveys concern relatively short-term effects of university research (that is, within twenty years). Although concerns about short-term effects fuel the current policy debate, the long-term effects of university research on technical advancement are clearly important but are not examined here. Because many suspect that these effects are considerable, omitting them is regrettable but unavoidable because of the dearth of systematic data on the subject.

The conventional view holds that the short-term impact of university research on industrial R&D is negligible except in a few industries.[4] Accumulating evidence suggests that we revise this perception. Studies published since 1989, as well as the results of the 1994 Carnegie Mellon Survey, suggest that university research provides critical short-term payoffs in some industries (such as pharmaceuticals) and is broadly important in numerous industries.

Klevorick, Levin, Nelson, and Winter conducted a 1983 survey of 650 R&D managers in 128 industries (with industries defined between the three- and four-digit SIC code levels). The researchers asked respondents to indicate on a seven-point Likert scale the relevance to their industry's technological progress of university research for each of eleven scientific and engineering disciplines.[5] The results largely confirmed conventional wisdom. Of the seventy-five industries for which the researchers received three or more responses, only fourteen (less than 20 percent) gave an average Likert score of at least four for any discipline. These fourteen industries were predominantly in the health or agricultural fields; but the list also included materials-based industries, scientific instruments, and semiconductors, among others.

One of the main conclusions of this effort is that university research was highly relevant to industrial R&D in some industries. Where its relevance was high, the most relevant discipline usually was either an engineering or applied science discipline rather than a basic science. In a few technology areas, basic sciences (particularly biological sciences) made a clear contribution—as in the creation of drugs. The overall conclusion was that university research findings made an important contribution in few industries and only a modest contribution in still a minority of other industries.

The findings from the 1984 survey by Blumenthal and others of 110 biotechnology firms were consistent with the 1983 survey by Klevorick and others[6] since biotechnology falls largely into one of the few domains, drugs, where the latter found the role of university research to be critical to industrial R&D. The survey by Blumenthal and others indicated that 46 percent of their sample firms supported university research, suggesting that a significant percentage of firms in biotechnology recognize its importance. The authors of the survey also found that university research produced a comparable number of patents per R&D dollar to the firms' own in-house research.

Another, more recent survey by Blumenthal and others obtained qualitatively similar results for a sample of firms spanning more industries.[7] In a 1994 survey of large firms in the life sciences industries (defined as including agriculture, chemicals, and drugs), they found that 59 percent of the firms supported research in universities. Moreover, more than 60 percent of the firms supporting university research received patents on products as a consequence of their relationships with universities.

Mansfield's survey of seventy-six firms spanned even more industries, including information processing, electrical equipment, and instrument, drug, metal, and oil firms.[8] Respondents estimated that for the period 1975–85, 10 percent of new products and processes would have been "substantially delayed" in the absence of "recent" academic research, where "recent academic research" refers to research conducted within the prior fifteen years, and a "substantial delay" refers to one of a year or more. Of the surveyed industries, three (namely chemicals other than drugs, oil, and electrical) fell well below the average of 10 percent. Mansfield estimated that this 10 percent of new products and processes that would have been substantially delayed accounted for $24 billion in sales in 1985. On the basis of these data and estimates of the lags associated with the commercial effects of academic R&D, Mansfield estimated that the annual social rate of return to investment in academic research during 1975–78 was 28 percent.

Mansfield's survey findings and analysis highlight two important points. They suggest that the short-term effects of academic research may be more widespread than commonly thought. However tentative his analysis of the economic returns to academic R&D may be, it also shows that, though the effect of academic R&D may appear small relative to the level of economic activity more generally (for example, it affected "only" 10 percent of sales), its absolute effect and the associated returns to academic R&D may be quite large.[9]

Rather than employ survey research methods, in two studies Jaffe and Adams employ regression analyses in a production function framework to evaluate the impact of academic research on technical advance.[10] Employing state-level aggregations of industrial patenting activity and university R&D, Jaffe examines the effect of academic research on industrial patenting activity. Patents were classified in four broadly defined academic fields:

drugs, chemicals, electronics, and the mechanical arts. Jaffe finds evidence of geographically mediated effects of university research on industrial patenting activity—most strongly in drugs, but also in chemicals and electronics. For a range of industrial activity even broader (although more aggregate) than that represented in Mansfield's study, Jaffe observes an apparent influence of university R&D that, while strongest for drug-related R&D, is reasonably pervasive.[11]

In research covering almost the entire U.S. manufacturing sector (that is, eighteen of the twenty two-digit SIC manufacturing industries), Adams estimates the effects of academic R&D on manufacturing productivity and the lags associated with those effects. He found the effects to be important and pervasive.[12] Adams estimated that the time required for academic research in the basic sciences to affect industrial productivity is twenty years, but for applied sciences and engineering the lag is between zero and ten years.[13]

The 1994 Carnegie Mellon Survey (CMS) of 1,478 R&D lab managers in the U.S. manufacturing sector suggests that the short-run effects of university research on industrial R&D are widespread.[14] In contrast with the results Klevorick and others obtained from data gathered in 1983, the CMS indicates that in two-thirds of the U.S. manufacturing industries surveyed, R&D managers estimated on average that academic research in at least one field was at least "moderately important" to their R&D activities (that is, scoring at least a three on a four-point Likert scale).[15] As shown in table 7-1, the survey also found that for the manufacturing sector overall, 15 percent of R&D projects are reported as using university research. Although the question is phrased differently from Mansfield's, this figure is nonetheless consistent with the findings for his more restricted sample.

The percentage of R&D projects using university research varies substantially across industries. For eight of the thirty-four industries, respondents report that 20 percent or more of their R&D projects use university research. These industries include petroleum refining, food, drugs, miscellaneous chemicals (including specialty chemicals), steel, semiconductors, search and navigation equipment, and aerospace. This list of industries not only

Table 7-1. *Form of Academic Outputs Used in Industrial R&D[a]*
Mean

| Industry | N | Percentage of industrial R&D projects using academic output by form of output | | |
		Research	Prototypes	Instruments
1500:Food	93	19.57	6.72	14.52
1700:Textiles	23	5.44	4.35	5.44
2100:Paper	30	17.33	5.83	15.00
2200:Printing/publishing	12	10.42	4.17	10.42
2320:Petroleum	15	24.67	1.67	11.33
2400:Chemicals	65	11.92	3.46	8.85
2411:Basic chemicals	37	12.84	1.35	8.78
2413:Plastic resins	28	7.14	0.89	8.93
2423:Drugs	52	32.40	9.14	17.31
2429:Miscellaneous chemicals	29	20.35	6.90	15.52
2500:Rubber/plastic	34	10.29	5.15	8.82
2600:Mineral products	19	14.21	2.63	9.21
2610:Glass	6	16.67	8.33	16.67
2695:Concrete, cement, lime	10	7.50	2.50	12.50
2700:Metal	8	18.75	3.13	12.50
2710:Steel	10	20.00	5.00	10.00
2800:Metal products	45	8.33	4.24	7.07
2910:General purpose machinery	76	10.20	6.84	7.24
2920:Special purpose machinery	68	14.34	6.18	8.75
2922:Machine tools	10	12.50	5.00	2.50
3010:Computers	22	12.50	1.14	11.36
3100:Electrical equipment	22	6.82	5.68	4.55
3110:Motor/generator	21	10.71	1.19	3.57
3130:Wiring	3	0.00	0.00	0.00
3210:Electronic components	26	14.42	7.69	11.35
3211:Semiconductors and related equipment	19	23.68	3.95	11.11
3220:Communications equipment	34	16.03	5.15	8.09
3230:TV/radio	8	12.50	12.50	21.88
3311:Medical equipment	69	19.49	6.09	11.88
3312:Precision instruments	36	9.03	8.89	15.97
3314:Search/navigational equipment	38	20.40	5.26	11.84
3410:Car/truck	9	16.67	8.33	19.45

Table 7–1. *continued*

Mean

| Industry | N | Percentage of industrial R&D projects using academic output by form of output | | |
		Research	Prototypes	Instruments
3430:Autoparts	34	9.56	8.68	12.35
3530:Aerospace	49	22.45	8.16	13.78
3600:Other manufacturing	87	12.93	8.05	10.63
All	1,147	15.12	5.79	10.92

Source: W.M. Cohen, R.R. Nelson, and J. Walsh, "Links and Impacts: New Survey Results on the Influence of University Research on Industrial R&D," Carnegie Mellon University, 1996.

[a]Computed using 0 percent for response category 0–10 percent. Otherwise used midpoint means for the following response categories: (1) 11 to 40 percent; (2) 41 to 60 percent; (3) 61 to 90 percent; (4) 91 to 100 percent.

includes high-technology industries (semiconductors, drugs, and medical equipment) but also industries typically considered to be mature (petroleum refining and steel).

Another finding of the Carnegie Mellon Survey (CMS), consistent with the earlier arguments posed in studies by Rosenberg and others, is that industrial R&D labs use research techniques and instrumentation developed in universities.[16] Examples are magnetic resonance imaging (MRI) and recombinant DNA research. As reported in table 7-1 for manufacturing overall, respondents report that 11 percent of industrial projects make use of techniques or instrumentation developed in universities. Again, cross-industry differences are significant. Fifteen percent or more of industrial R&D projects are reported to use techniques and instrumentation developed in universities in seven of thirty-four industries, including paper, drugs, miscellaneous chemicals (including specialty chemicals), glass, television and radio, precision instruments, and cars and trucks.

The CMS sheds light on how information from university research contributes to industrial R&D. One view of the role of university research, consistent with a long-standing conception of the role of basic research generally, is that it produces new ideas for industrial R&D projects.[17] University research also serves a second function, phrased in the survey as "contributing to the execution of existing R&D projects"—what may be called problem solving. This function could be seen as solving problems on how to do research. The survey finds that university research suggests new R&D projects and contributes to project execution almost comparably across the manufacturing sector, with the latter being a little more important. Again, however, there are significant cross-industry differences in the patterns regarding the role of university research. The CMS finds that university research contributes principally to problem-solving in medical equipment, search and navigation equipment, cars and trucks, and aerospace, among others. University research principally provides new R&D project ideas in petroleum refining, steel, machine tools, semiconductors, and precision instruments.

Another measure of the importance of university research to industrial R&D is provided by comparing its contribution with that of three other well-recognized extramural information sources: buyers, suppliers, and competitors (although with somewhat different effect). The CMS results indicate that universities do not have as important an effect as buyers and suppliers; however, universities are as significant a source of information as competitors. This finding is important in light of the wealth of empirical studies (surveyed by Griliches) that indicate that "R&D spillovers" from competitors make substantial contributions to technical advance and productivity growth within industries.[18] If universities are comparable in importance to competitors, they have a substantial effect on industrial R&D.

The Carnegie Mellon Survey provides valuable insights into how useful information moves from universities to industrial R&D facilities. To evaluate the importance of the different information channels with the CMS data, we computed the percentage of respondents indicating that a given channel is at least "moderately important." As shown in table 7-2, the four dominant channels of communication between university research and industrial R&D are publications (with 41 percent of respondents indicating that publications are at least "moderately important"), public meetings and conferences (34 percent), informal information channels (35 percent), and consulting (32 percent). A factor analysis indicates that these four information channels tend to be used together. This indicates that person-to-person interactions, such as informal information exchange or consulting, tend to be used with and complement more public channels, such as publications or conferences.[19] Other, less important channels of communication include recent hires, joint or cooperative ventures between industry and universities, patents, and contract research.

In summary, the recent CMS results suggest that academic R&D is central to technical advance in a small number of industries and is also broadly useful. This overall result (though consistent with more recent analyses) signals a change, particularly from the study by Klevorick and others, which based its results on a survey administered in 1983, eleven years before.[20] Why the change? There are a number of possible explanations.

First, the change may be real. One factor that could account for the growing influence of academic research across the manufacturing sector is deepening ties that have developed between universities and industry since 1980 (discussed below). These ties have been stimulated by an aggressive response by faculty and university administrations to shifts in policy surrounding the support of academic research. A complementary factor may be downsizing of central and typically more upstream industrial R&D activities, which is believed to have occurred over the past decade.[21] Downsizing may have induced firms to rely more on academics for the kind of research that they supported internally in the past.

A second possible explanation for the new findings is that the change is simply perceptual. According to this explanation, nothing has changed. However—perhaps due to the greater visibility of selected academic R&D activities in biotechnology, computer science, robotics, and the like—firms simply believe that academics are contributing more to industrial R&D.

A third possible explanation is that the new results reflect only different samples and a new survey instrument that poses both different questions and similar questions differently. This last possibility raises the question of which survey to believe. The CMS offers advantages leading one to conclude that it is more reliable. Rather than restrict itself exclusively to one question

Table 7-2. *Importance to Industrial R&D of Information Sources on University Research*

Percentage respondents indicating "moderately" or "very" important

	N	Patents	Pubs.	Meetings or conferences	Informal channels	Hires	Licenses	JV's	Contract research	Consulting	Personal exchange
1500:Food	92	9.78	51.09	38.04	43.48	21.74	10.87	22.83	29.35	46.74	7.61
1700:Textiles	23	13.04	26.09	26.09	21.74	21.74	0.00	13.04	8.70	13.04	0.00
2100:Paper	31	9.68	45.16	35.48	32.26	9.68	0.00	19.35	35.48	22.58	3.23
2200:Printing/publishing	12	16.67	33.33	25.00	16.67	8.33	8.33	0.00	16.67	25.00	0.00
2320:Petroleum	15	0.00	46.67	53.33	33.33	13.33	13.33	13.33	26.67	46.67	0.00
2400:Chemicals	64	25.00	34.37	28.12	18.75	18.75	7.81	15.62	20.63	26.56	9.37
2411:Basic chemicals	36	16.67	30.56	25.00	33.33	19.44	2.78	16.67	19.44	33.33	2.78
2413:Plastic resins	26	11.54	34.62	26.92	23.08	23.08	0.00	3.85	11.54	15.38	0.00
2423:Drugs	51	56.86	72.55	60.78	60.78	31.37	35.29	41.18	54.90	54.90	7.84
2429:Miscellaneous chemicals	29	27.59	37.93	27.59	31.03	24.14	3.45	3.45	13.79	24.14	0.00
2500:Rubber/plastic	34	5.88	17.65	14.71	8.82	14.71	2.94	11.76	8.82	20.59	0.00
2600:Mineral products	19	5.26	26.32	21.05	21.05	31.58	5.26	10.53	10.53	26.32	10.53
2610:Glass	6	33.33	50.00	50.00	50.00	50.00	16.67	50.00	33.33	33.33	0.00
2695:Concrete, cement, lime	10	30.00	50.00	30.00	20.00	30.00	30.00	50.00	10.00	10.00	10.00
2700:Metal	7	28.57	71.43	71.43	85.71	28.57	0.00	28.57	42.86	57.14	14.29
2710:Steel	11	18.18	36.36	54.55	45.45	18.18	18.18	36.36	54.55	36.36	18.18
2800:Metal products	47	21.28	27.66	14.89	25.53	19.15	8.51	14.89	10.64	23.40	4.26
2910:General purpose machinery	73	16.44	31.94	26.03	30.14	13.70	8.22	10.96	13.70	32.88	1.37
2920:Special purpose machinery	67	19.40	31.34	32.84	26.87	17.91	11.94	17.91	16.42	32.84	2.99
2922:Machine Tools	10	10.00	40.00	40.00	40.00	20.00	0.00	10.00	20.00	40.00	0.00
3010:Computers	24	8.33	41.67	41.67	33.33	33.33	4.17	8.33	8.33	29.17	4.17
3100:Electrical Equipment	22	9.09	31.82	22.73	22.73	0.00	0.00	9.09	13.64	9.09	0.00

3110:Motor/Generator	22	4.55	40.91	36.36	45.45	13.64	0.00	22.73	13.64	31.82	4.55
3210:Electronic Components	25	20.00	36.00	28.00	36.00	32.00	12.00	12.00	8.00	33.33	4.00
3211:Semiconductors and Related Equipment	18	22.22	61.11	55.56	64.71	27.78	16.67	27.78	16.67	33.33	5.56
3220:Communications Equipment	34	5.88	50.00	32.35	32.35	29.41	8.82	8.82	17.65	29.41	20.59
3230:TV/Radio	8	25.00	75.00	37.50	37.50	25.00	12.50	37.50	25.00	25.00	12.50
3311:Medical Equipment	69	27.54	37.68	34.78	46.38	18.84	18.84	23.19	23.19	44.93	5.80
3312:Precision Instruments	36	25.00	50.00	44.44	44.44	11.11	13.89	19.44	8.33	36.11	5.56
3314:Search/Navigational Equipment	37	5.41	51.35	48.65	48.65	21.62	13.51	29.73	35.14	43.24	13.51
3410:Car/Truck	9	33.33	33.33	11.11	33.33	11.11	11.11	22.22	33.33	22.22	11.11
3430:Autoparts	32	9.37	43.75	31.25	25.00	18.75	9.37	21.87	18.75	21.87	9.37
3530:Aerospace	48	14.58	58.33	50.00	54.17	18.75	6.25	39.58	35.42	39.58	4.17
3600:Other Manufacturing	83	13.25	33.73	33.73	32.53	18.07	6.02	10.84	18.07	21.69	8.43
All	1,130	17.61	40.91	34.42	35.28	19.91	9.73	18.49	21.26	32.15	5.84

Source: Cohen, Nelson, and Walsh, "Links and Impacts."

using subjective response categories defined along a Likert scale, the CMS poses numerous questions on the subject, most of which provided objective response categories. Moreover, in the process, the CMS forced respondents to think about the contribution of university research in tangible ways.

Effects of Industrial Ties on Academic Research

This section considers the impact of these deepening ties with industry on academic research, specifically on its composition and public dissemination. Although this is of interest for its own sake, the composition and dissemination of university R&D also may have important implications for technological progress in the long run.

The relationship between university research and industry has deepened substantially since the mid-1970s. There were an estimated 1,056 university-industry R&D centers in the United States as of 1990.[22] One survey indicates that although the first of these centers was established in the 1880s, almost 60 percent were established between 1980 and 1989. Moreover, the magnitude of R&D activity performed by these centers is substantial. These centers spent an estimated total of $4.1 billion in 1990, with $2.9 billion spent on R&D. This is more than double the National Science Foundation's $1.3 billion in support for all academic R&D in 1990, and almost one-fifth of all U.S. academic R&D expenditures in science and engineering.

Another indicator that university research is moving closer to the commercial sector is academic patenting activity. In 1974, 177 patents were awarded to the top 100 research universities. In 1984, that number increased to 408, and in 1994 it jumped dramatically to 1,486 patents.[23] Related to this increase in university patenting activity, gross royalties from licenses have also increased. According to a survey conducted by the Association of University Technology Managers, gross royalties from licenses from 101 surveyed universities grew from $163 million in 1991 to $318 million by 1994.[24] The formation of university offices administering technology transfer and licensing also reflects growing ties between industry and university research. In 1980, twenty-five American universities had such offices; by 1990, the number had grown to 200.[25]

The share of academic R&D supported by industry has also increased. Although government still supports the bulk of academic R&D, the share accounted for by industry more than doubled between 1970 and 1990. In 1970 the industry share of support for academic R&D was 2.6 percent. That share grew to 3.9 percent in 1980 and 6.9 percent in 1990. Moreover, we estimate that about half of industry support for academic R&D actually went to university-industry R&D centers in 1990.[26] Although we have no systematic data on either spin-offs or faculty participation in new firms, the anecdotal evidence indicates an increase over the past fifteen years, particularly in biotechnology and software. A related development over the past five years—again, one that is not well documented—is the growing number of instances in which universities hold equity stakes in firms that are spun off to commercialize innovations originating from the universities' research.[27]

Any consideration of the impact of these deepening ties with industry on academic research requires an understanding of the impetus behind those relationships, the reasons such relationships emerged, and the broader incentives of the parties involved. The impetus behind increased industry support for university research comes primarily from universities, not industry. Consistent with Etzkowitz's argument that a norm of entrepreneurialism has diffused across research universities, the results presented in table 7-3 indicate that 73 percent of university-industry research centers (UIRCs) were established because of an immediate impetus originating from universities.[28] A breakdown of that 73 percent figure shows that 61 percent were the result of an impetus from faculty and 12 percent of an impetus from university administrations. Government provided the impetus for approximately 11 percent of these centers, and industry provided it for approximately 11 percent. The funds for university-industry R&D centers, however, come principally from government, not from industry, with government providing 46 percent and industry 31 percent of the funds per center, on average, in 1990.[29]

Table 7-3. *Sources of Immediate Impetus behind Center Formation*

Source	Percentage of centers
University	
Faculty	60.9
Administration	11.6
Government	10.9
Industry	10.7
Other	5.9

Source: W.M. Cohen, R. Florida, and L. Randazzese, *For Knowledge and Profit: University-Industry R&D Centers in the United States* (Oxford University Press, forthcoming).

The important and obvious question is, why have the links between industry and universities strengthened since the late 1970s? In light of this discussion, the underlying issue is why faculty are seeking support from industry more aggressively than they had before. The reason is the money, of course, but why now? Academics apparently have felt the need to search for sources of support other than government since 1980 as a result of changes in the policy environment.

The first important change in policy is that competition for federal support has increased since the mid-1970s. Between 1979 and 1991, although the absolute level of federal spending on university research increased, federal support per academic researcher declined.[30] Specifically, federal funding per full time academic scientist active in R&D fell by 9.4 percent in real terms. Moreover, the federal share of academic R&D dropped from 69 percent in 1973 to 58 percent in 1991.[31]

The second policy change is a shift in government attitudes toward collaborations between industry and universities. Prompted largely by growing international competition, legislative changes have encouraged academics to solicit support from industry and have also given industry an incentive to be more forthcoming. Specifically, the Economic Recovery Tax Act of 1981 extended industrial R&D tax breaks to support research at universities. In addition, since the 1970s there has been substantial growth in government programs (such as the NSF's Science and Technology Centers and Engineering Research Centers) that tie government support for university research to industry participation.

Third, policy has changed regarding the ability of universities to profit from their research. The Patent and Trademark Act of 1980, otherwise known as Bayh-Dole, permits universities and other nonprofit institutions to obtain patent rights to the products of federally sponsored research. This legislation permits universities to profit from federal research projects both directly and by assigning patent rights to others, frequently industrial cosponsors.

In addition to understanding the institutional reasons for the deepening ties between industry and universities, it is also helpful to understand the broader incentives of the parties involved. First, consider the firms. They want to profit from the fruits of their support for university research, namely from new or improved processes or products made possible by university research. The immediate outputs of supported research do not necessarily take tangible form, such as inventions, patents, or prototypes. Rather, they often are "intermediate outcomes"—essentially pieces of intangible knowledge that help firms conduct their R&D more efficiently, suggest ideas for new projects, or open up whole new domains for research.[32] Intermediate knowledge outcomes may be transferred to the firm in numerous ways, including papers, informal interactions, hiring of students, and so on.

On the university side of the relationship are two parties, administration and faculty. University administrators appear to be interested chiefly in the revenue generated by relationships with industry. The faculty, who tend to be the prime movers behind these relationships, have two motives.[33] They undoubtedly desire support, per se, because it contributes to their personal incomes (such as by providing summer support or by making them more desirable on the academic market) and allows them to do the research they want to do. In addition, and with important implications for faculty-industry interactions, industry support assists faculty members in conducting research that allows them to achieve academic eminence. Eminence is achieved primarily through foundational research that provides the building blocks for other research and therefore tends to be widely cited. The free and open disclosure of research that provides for its broad dissemination is essential to the achievement of eminence.

The academic quest for eminence, involving the open disclosure of foundational research, conflicts with the profit incentive of
firms.[34] Firms tend to be less interested in foundational research
because it typically does not address their needs and concerns in
a direct, usable way. Firms also prefer less disclosure of research
findings to increase the appropriability of the profits of any process or product innovations that may grow out of the research. As
highlighted by Dasgupta and David, this conflict between the
incentives for academics and those for firms suggests that to
secure industry support or otherwise to conduct research for
commercial gain, faculty may be induced to shift to more applied
research and restrict the disclosure of their research findings.[35]

Consider the evidence that industry support shifts academic
research away from more basic research to more applied research
and development. In studying the life sciences industry, Blumenthal and others find that industry-supported research tends to be
short term.[36] Survey research studies by Rahm and Morgan find
an empirical association between greater faculty interaction with
industry and more applied research.[37] As shown in table 7-4, the
survey of university-industry R&D centers (UIRCs) found that
the mission of improving industry's products and processes is
indeed associated with a declining share of UIRC effort going
toward basic research.[38] Specifically, centers that attach little or no
importance to that mission devote 61 percent of their effort to
basic research, in contrast with 29 percent of the R&D effort of
centers that consider the mission of improving industry's products and processes to be "very important."

Though this evidence may appear compelling, it is inconclu-
sive. It is unclear whether pressure from industry (or, similarly,
the lure of personal commercial gain) induces academics to
change their research agendas, or whether faculty who are already doing more applied research simply attract more support
from industry. This latter possibility is suggested by National
Science Board data showing that the composition of academic
R&D over the past fifteen years has been relatively stable.[39] NSB
data show that the fraction of university R&D dedicated to basic
research was 67 percent during 1980–83 and 66 percent during
1990–93. For 1994–95, the NSB estimates that universities devoted

Table 7-4. *Effects of Industrial Orientation on Research Effort*

Share of research	Research			N
	Basic	Applied	Development	
Entire sample	41.0	42.1	16. 8	496
Centers distinguished by priority attached to mission of improving industry's products or processes				
Not important	61.2	35.5	3.2	66
Somewhat important	39.0	46.6	14.4	130
Important	38.3	42.2	19.5	162
Very important	28.9	42.6	28.4	122

Source: Cohen, Florida, and Randazzese, *For Knowledge and Profit.*

approximately 67 percent of their R&D effort to basic research. In 1970–73, the NSB reports that 77 percent of university R&D effort was dedicated to basic research, indicating that the reorientation of university R&D away from basic research largely predated the significant strengthening of university-industry ties that began in the mid-1970s and picked up steam in the 1980s. In any event, since 1980, universities have apparently not changed the composition of their research much, despite growing links with industry and the commercial sector. Thus, perhaps industry money for university research was attracted by the applied component of university research that had already emerged prior to any increase in industry support or interest.

Though still limited, the evidence that growing ties with industry are inducing academics to accept restrictions on the disclosure of their research is more persuasive. Recent anecdotal evidence is strong. For example, based on a *New England Journal of Medicine* article by Stephen Rosenberg, chief surgeon and leading investigator of the National Cancer Institute, the *New York Times* reported: "In recent years, going against a long tradition of openness in science, many researchers have accepted secrecy as a common working practice. This change is impeding progress in cancer research and other fields. The trend toward secrecy . . . has grown . . . as competition for federal science grants has increased and more scientists have come to rely on grants or contracts from private companies that are investing in biomedical research."[40] Likewise, the *Wall Street Journal* reported that one drug company suppressed findings from research that it supported at the University of California at San Francisco. The research found that cheaper drugs made by other manufacturers were therapeutically effective substitutes for its drug, Synthroid, which dominates the $600 million market for drugs to control hypothyroidism.[41]

More broad-based quantitative evidence also signals a relationship between disclosure restrictions and industry support. Blumenthal and others report that 82 percent of the companies they surveyed that support life science research within universities require academic researchers to keep information confidential to allow for the filing of a patent application, but they further report that 47 percent of firms indicate that their agreements with universities occasionally require academic institutions to keep confidential the results of the sponsored research longer than is necessary to file a patent application. In a yet more recent survey research study Blumenthal and others find that, while withholding research results is not particularly widespread among life science researchers generally, "Participation in the commercialization of research, which can occur with or without support from industry, is associated with both delays in publication and refusal to share research results upon request."[42]

In similar survey research, Rahm asked 1,134 university technology managers and faculty at the 100 top R&D performing universities in the United States about the extent of communication and publication restrictions that the firms they deal with seek to impose.[43] Thirty-nine percent of the technology managers indicated that, in order to protect the secrecy of a potential commercial product, the firms they have dealt with have placed restrictions on faculty sharing information regarding R&D breakthroughs with department or center faculty. Seventy-nine percent of the technology managers and 53 percent of the faculty with experience interacting with firms reported that firms had asked for R&D results to be delayed or kept from publication.

The survey conducted by Cohen, Florida, and Goe examined UIRC policies regarding restrictions placed on publication and informal communication.[44] As shown in table 7-5, 53 percent of university-industry R&D centers permit firms to request publication delays, and 35 percent allow "information to be deleted from research papers prior to submission for publication."[45] Of the 117

Table 7-5. *Research Disclosure Policies of Centers*

Percent (unless otherwise specified)

	Information can be deleted from publication	Publication can be delayed	Both restrictions	N
Entire sample	34.8	52.5	31.1	496
Centers distinguishecd by priority attached to mission of improving industry's products or processses				
Not important	20.9	48.8	19.4	66
Somewhat important	22.9	46.6	19.8	130
Important	37.7	55.3	33.3	162
Very important	53.9	63.2	48.7	122

Source: Cohen, Florida, and Randazzese, *For Knowledge and Profit.*

centers in the sample that strongly embraced the mission of improving industry's products or processes (that is, that indicated this mission to be "very important"), 63 percent permit publication delays, and 54 percent permit the deletion of information from prospective publications.[46]

This same survey asked respondents whether center faculty and staff are ever restricted in sharing information about their projects with others, including other faculty and staff within their home universities, faculty and staff at other institutions, and the general public. The results, presented in table 7-6, are broadly consistent with those bearing on publication restrictions. Across all centers in the sample, 21 percent report communication restrictions with other faculty and staff within the home university, 29 percent report restrictions with faculty and staff at other universities, and 42 percent report restrictions with the general public. For centers that consider the mission of improving industry's products or processes to be "very important," 37 percent report communication restrictions with other faculty or staff at the home university, 46 percent with faculty or staff at other universities, and 55 percent with the general public.[47]

Our consideration of the impacts of deepening ties with industry on the conduct and disclosure of academic research has been limited to the case where established firms provide research support to the university. We have not considered faculty participation in firms or the formation of new firms by academies (that

Table 7-6. *Communication Restrictions*

Percent (unless otherwise specified)

If center personnel are ever restricted in sharing project-related information with:	Other faculty and staff within the university	Faculty and staff at other universities	General public	N
Entire sample	21.3	28.6	41.5	479
Centers distinguished by priority attached to mission of improving industry's products or processes				
Not important	8.1	11.3	17.7	62
Somewhat important	16.9	21	37.1	124
Important	19.1	27.4	43.9	157
Very important	37.2	46.3	55.4	121

Source: Cohen, Florida, and Randazzese, *For Knowlege and Profit*.

is, spin-offs). As we have noted, spin-offs from universities appear to have increased over the past fifteen years, especially in the domains of biotechnology and computer science, but we are not aware of any systematic data on the subject. The relevant issue is the implications of spin-offs for the empirical conclusions of this section. A priori, the prospect or existence of a spin-off company that capitalizes on academic research should impose pressures on the composition and disclosure of research qualitatively similar to those associated with industry support for academic research. The main difference in this case is that those pressures are internally generated by the faculty or university administrator, rather than externally induced. The National Science Board data indicating that the composition of U.S. academic research has been relatively stable since 1980 suggest that if there has been a proliferation of spin-off activity since that time, it has not affected the percentage of basic research performed in universities.48 Without data, however, it is hard to know if spin-off activity has had the same apparent effect in increasing disclosure restrictions as industry support.

University-Industry Relationships and Technological Change

The evidence strongly suggests that universities contribute substantially to industrial R&D, that ties between universities and industry have grown, and that industry support in academic research is bringing greater restrictions on the disclosure of the results of university R&D. It is worth reflecting on possible implications of these trends for technological change.

On balance, the impacts of these deepening ties on technical advances are not obvious. The survey cited previously underscores the countervailing effects of these ties.[49] Specifically, for the sort of UIRC R&D outputs of more immediate value to industry (such as new processes, and new products), UIRC R&D productivity appears to be greater for centers that embrace the mission of improving industry's products and processes more strongly.[50] Controlling for technology, productivity per researcher, measured by inventions disclosed, patent applications, new products or new processes, is 25 percent higher in centers that report the mission to improve industry's products and processes to be very important than it is for centers that consider this mission to be unimportant. With some notable exceptions, as in biotechnology, there is a parallel decline in academic paper productivity (also by roughly 25 percent) as the importance of that industry mission increases. These results suggest that the most commercially oriented UIRCs have a greater short-term effect on technical advance but a countervailing effect in the long run, particularly in light of findings by Adams that academic papers contribute to technical advances.[51]

Although the UIRC productivity data are ambiguous with respect to whether technical advance will suffer (or prosper) in the long run as a result of closer integration of industry and academic research, they reflect only the narrow experience of UIRCs themselves. They tell us little about the diminution in technical advance that might accompany blocking the information channels that benefit the R&D of firms not participating in the UIRCs. From this broader perspective, the findings that restrictive policies often accompany the strengthening of university-industry research ties are unsettling.[52]

Increased disclosure restrictions have several effects. First, they compromise the norm of open science valued by researchers as an end in itself. More importantly, disclosure restrictions undermine the quality of academic research by diminishing the extent to which research methods and results are subjected to professional review and criticism. Moreover, by preventing results from entering the public domain, restrictions both increase wasteful duplication of research efforts and reduce the likelihood that research will contribute to further work, and may thus impede the cumulative advance of science and engineering. Disclosure restrictions also have broader effects than undermining the advance of academic research. Open disclosure underpins the university's contribution to industrial R&D and technical advance more generally. Recall the findings regarding the channels through which university research influences industrial R&D. Disclosure through publications and public meetings and conferences was found to complement more interactive channels, such as informal communication and consulting. Together, these channels appear to play the key role in transferring knowledge and technology from university to industry.

Disclosure restrictions thus apparently block the most important media through which universities contribute to technical advance. Though firms that directly team up with academic researchers will still presumably benefit from university research subject to disclosure restrictions, the more diffuse, decentralized benefits realized by other firms and industry generally will not be forthcoming. To the extent that these restrictions proliferate, even the firms granted these restricted information channels may suffer in the long run by diminishing the publicly available information that benefits them as well as others.

One countervailing influence to the disclosure restrictions is the spillovers from the downstream R&D conducted by firms that benefit from these restrictions. These spillovers are not likely to fully substitute for the information flows initially blocked for several reasons. First, firms will try to restrict spillovers to retain proprietary advantage. The subsequent revelation of the underlying knowledge also will be limited because it will tend to be conveyed indirectly—as, for example, through its embodiment in some product. Finally, there will typically be considerable lags between when the firm receives the privileged information and when information will spill over to other firms.

Industry's restriction of public disclosure of university research may thus undermine the long-term interest of industry itself, no less the consumers who benefit from industry's new and improved products and process. The challenge is that posed by the decentralized provision of many public goods. The argument through which one might see a "tragedy of the commons" unfolding begins with the recognition that, given the option, it will rarely be in the interest of any one firm providing support to academic R&D to eschew some form of disclosure restriction. The firm will see a tangible benefit in restricting public disclosure of the research—a benefit that comes from denying its rivals access to that research. At the same time, with little reason to believe that its behavior will have much effect on that of others, the firm will expect that the effect on its own profits from diminishing the pool of publicly accessible information is imperceptible. As a consequence, the expected private benefit of a restriction will far outweigh the expected cost.

This argument and the empirical findings that underpin it suggest that the conventional public good argument for government intervention may apply to the question of disclosure restrictions. Government cannot and should not compel firms to support university research if firms do not find it in their interests to do so, and a key dimension of those interests may include restricting the disclosure of research findings. Moreover, it is not even industry that is driving the formation of most of these relationships, but the academy itself—providing all the more reason why firms cannot be compelled to support academic research from which they cannot profit.

One policy that would pull all concerned parties out of what may be collectively self-defeating behavior is public financial support of university research sufficient to obviate the need for industry support. In the current fiscal environment, such support is not likely to be forthcoming. Moreover, strong public support may also undermine some of the potentially important benefits—including the tangible contributions of universities to technical advance—that appear to accompany those ties. We should also not underestimate the effect that such ties have in altering university research agendas in socially useful ways by making university scientists and engineers more aware of the technical problems and opportunities confronting industry. The challenge, then, is to preserve the benefits of industrial ties while minimizing the most significant cost, namely, the imposition of disclosure restrictions. One policy option is to tie the tax benefit that firms receive for supporting university R&D to the disclosure of the supported research findings.

Another policy alternative would not involve government intervention of any sort. Academics may accede to more restrictive policies than are necessary as a consequence of having little bargaining power when the firms know that the faculty need research support and have few or no alternatives. The leverage academics hold may be strengthened if, during their negotiations with firms, they could invoke strong guidelines for research disclosure. Individual universities or research universities collectively could create such guidelines and could even back them up by monitoring the disclosure restrictions that come with industry support.

The issue of disclosure is clearly a sensitive one—surely one of degree and involving trade-offs. We should not allow the deepening of ties between academia and industry to undermine the norms and practices that benefit both the private sector and society in general. But there are no villains in this story. Industry and faculty alike are responding to their evolving constraints and incentives in legitimate ways. In the process, if we are not at least endangering one of the geese of golden egg fame, we may yet be undermining its habitat. Due care should be exercised to preserve it.

Endnotes

1. Although these controversies have intensified in the past fifteen years, they are not new. Weiner, for example, documents that there has been controversy in the field of biomedicine since the early twentieth century between those who wished to patent inventions originating from university labs versus those who thought such patenting was in conflict with making medical discoveries available for public use and further development. Charles Weiner, "Patenting and Academic Research: Historical Case Studies," in Vivian Weil and John W. Snapper,

eds., *Owning Scientific and Technical Information: Value and Ethical Issues* (Rutgers University Press, 1989).

2. The full results of this study are forthcoming: Wesley Cohen, Richard Florida, and Lucien Randazzese, *For Knowledge and Profit: University-Industry R&D Centers in the United States* (Oxford University Press, forthcoming).

3. The complete results reporting this survey's findings on the effects of academic research on industrial R&D are presented in Wesley M. Cohen, Richard Nelson, and John Walsh, "Links and Impacts: New Survey Results on the Influence of University Research on Industrial R&D," Carnegie Mellon University, Department of Social and Decision Sciences, 1996.

4. A. K. Klevorick and others, "On the Sources and Significance of Interindustry Differences in Technological Opportunities," *Research Policy*, vol. 24, no. 2 (1994), pp. 195–206.

5. For purposes of comparison, it is important to recall that, although these results from the survey by Klevorick and others were not published until 1994, the survey was conducted in 1983.

6. David Blumenthal and others, "Industrial Support of University Research in Biotechnology," *Science*, vol. 231 (January 17, 1986), pp. 242–46; and Klevorick and others, "On the Sources and Significance of Interindustry Differences."

7. David Blumenthal and others, "Relationships between Academic Institutions and Industry in the Life Sciences—An Industry Survey," *New England Journal of Medicine*, vol. 334, no. 6 (February 8, 1996), pp. 368–73.

8. Edwin Mansfield, "Academic Research and Industrial Innovation," *Research Policy*, vol. 20, no. 1 (February 1991), pp. 1–12.

9. Edwin Mansfield, "Academic Research and Industrial Innovation: A Further Note," *Research Policy*, vol. 21, no. 3 (June 1992), pp. 295–96.

10. Adam B. Jaffe, "Real Effects of Academic Research," *American Economic Review*, vol. 79, no. 5 (December 1989), pp. 957–78; and James D. Adams, "Fundamental Stocks of Knowledge and Productivity Growth," *Journal of Political Economy*, vol. 98, no. 4 (August 1990), pp. 673–702.

11. Jaffe, "Real Effects of Academic Research."

12. Adams, "Fundamental Stocks of Knowledge."

13. Because the effect of the basic sciences on industrial productivity often moves indirectly through applied sciences and engineering, the lags associated with some research in the basic sciences may be considerably less than twenty years. Cf. Nathan Rosenberg and Richard Nelson, "American Universities and Technical Advance in Industry," *Research Policy*, vol. 23, no. 3 (May 1994), pp. 323–48.

14. Cohen, Nelson, and Walsh, "Links and Impacts."

15. Klevorick and others, "On the Sources and Significance of Inter-industry Differences."

16. Nathan Rosenberg, "Scientific Instrumentation and University Research," *Research Policy*, vol. 21 (1992), pp. 381–90.

17. Vannevar Bush, *Science, the Endless Frontier: A Report to the President* (Government Printing Office, 1945).

18. Zvi Griliches, "The Search for R&D Spillovers," Working Paper 3768 (Cambridge, Mass.: National Bureau of Economic Research, 1991). What economists call within-industry "R&D spillovers" essentially reflect useful knowledge flows that firms receive about the R&D activities of their rivals without paying their rivals for them.

19. In an earlier study of information usage in technological innovation, Gibbons and Johnston similarly found that the two sources of "personal contact" and the technical literature contributed significantly to industrial innovation. See Michael Gibbons and Ron Johnston, "The Roles of Science in Technological Innovation," *Research Policy*, vol. 3 (1975), pp. 220–42. Also resembling the Carnegie Mellon Survey results, Gibbons and Johnston found these two types of sources to be most beneficial when used together. They state, "the use of the two general sources in tandem led to new and relevant information which would have been very difficult to obtain in any other way" (p. 34). Faulkner and Senker confirm this finding in a recent study of public sector research and industrial innovation in biotechnology, engineering ceramics, and parallel computing. Wendy Faulkner and Jacqueline Senker, *Knowledge Frontiers: Public Sector Research and Industrial Innovation in Biotechnology, Engineering Ceramics, and Parallel Computing* (Oxford University Press, 1995).

20. Jaffe, "Real Effects of Academic Research"; Mansfield, "Academic Research and Industrial Innovation"; Adams, "Fundamental Stocks of Knowledge"; and Klevorick and others, "On the Sources and Significance of Interindustry Differences."

21. David A. Hounshell, "The Evolution of Industrial Research in the United States," in Richard S. Rosenbloom and William J. Spencer, eds., *Engines of Innovation* (Boston: Harvard Business School Press, 1996), pp. 13–86; and Richard S. Rosenbloom and William J. Spencer, "Technology's Vanishing Wellspring," in Rosenbloom and Spencer, eds., *Engines of Innovation*, pp. 1–9.

22. Wesley M. Cohen, Richard Florida, and W. Richard Goe, *University–Industry Research Centers in the United States*, report prepared for the Ford Foundation (Pittsburgh: Carnegie Mellon University, June 1994).

23. National Science Board, *Science and Engineering Indicators*, NSB Pub. 96–21 (1996), table 5–42, p. 249.

24. Association of University Technology Managers, Inc., "AUTM Licensing Survey Fiscal Year 1991–Fiscal Year 1994," (Norwalk, Conn., 1995), p. 5.

25. AUTM, "Licensing Survey."

26. Cohen, Florida, and Randazzese, *For Knowledge and Profit.*

27. Hsu recommends that universities use this strategy to profit from their patents. Richard C. Hsu, "No Money for Research? Try Investing," *New York Times,* September 29, 1996, pp. F12.

28. Henry Etzkowitz, "Entrepreneurial Science in the Academy: A Case of the Transformation of Norms," *Social Problems,* vol. 36, no. 1 (1989), pp. 14–29; and Cohen, Florida, and Randazzese, *For Knowledge and Profit.*

29. The balance of the funding comes from the universities themselves (18 percent), private foundations (3 percent), and other sources. Cohen, Florida, and Randazzese, *For Knowledge and Profit.*

30. Harvey Brooks and Lucien Randazzese, "Universities-Industry Relations: The Next Four Years and Beyond," in Lewis Branscomb and James Keller, eds., *Investing in Innovation: Creating a Research and Innovation Policy That Works* (MIT Press, forthcoming). Brooks and Randazzese indicate that this figure is calculated from National Science Board, *Science and Engineering Indicators,* Appendix tables 5–2 and 5–26, and also highlight that the price deflator used to calculate it is the consumer price index, which tends to understate R&D cost increases over time, suggesting that the 9.4 percent figure is probably an underestimate of the actual decline.

31. National Science Board, *Science and Engineering Indicators.*

32. W. M. Cohen, R. Florida, and R. Goe, "University-Industry Research Centers in the United States," report to the Ford Foundation, Carnegie Mellon University, 1994.

33. Wesley M. Cohen and Lucien Randazzese, "Eminence and Enterprise: The Impact of Industry Support on the Conduct of Academic Research in Science and Engineering," Carnegie Mellon University, August 1996.

34. Robert K. Merton, *The Sociology of Science: Theoretical and Empirical Investigations* (University of Chicago Press, 1973); Partha Dasgupta and Paul David, "Information Disclosure and the Economics of Science and Technology," in George R. Feiwel, ed., *Arrow and the Ascent of Modern Economic Theory* (New York University Press, 1987); and Partha Dasgupta and Paul David, "Toward a New Economics of Science," Stanford University, Center for Economic Policy Research, 1992.

35. Dasgupta and David, "Information Disclosure and the Economics of Science and Technology"; and Dasgupta and David, "Toward a New Economics of Science."

36. Blumenthal and others, "Relationships between Academic Institutions and Industry."

37. Dianne Rahm, "University-Firm Linkages for Industrial Innovation," paper prepared for the Center for Economic Policy Re-

search/AAAS Conference on University Goals, Institutional Mecha-
nisms and the "Industrial Transferability of Research," 1994; Robert P.
Morgan and others, "Engineering Research in U.S. Universities: How
Engineering Faculty View It," paper prepared for the 1993 Institute of
Electrical and Electronics Engineers–American Society of Electrical Engi-
neers (IEEE-ASEE) Frontiers in Education Conference; and Robert P.
Morgan and others, "Engineering Research in U.S. Universities: How
University-Based Research Directors See It," paper prepared for the 1994
annual meeting of the American Society of Electrical Engineers.

38. Cohen, Florida, and Goe, "University-Industry Research Centers in the United States."

39. National Science Board, *Science and Engineering Indicators*.

40. Lawrence K. Altman, "Medical Research Is Hurt by Secrecy,
Official Says," *New York Times*, February 10, 1996, sec. 1, p. 9.

41. Ralph T. King Jr., "Bitter Pill: How a Drug Firm Paid for University Study, Then Undermined It," *Wall Street Journal*, April 25, 1996, pp.
pp. A1, A13.

42. David Blumenthal and others, "Withholding Research Results
in Academic Life Science: Evidence from a National Survey of Faculty,"
Journal of the American Medical Association, vol. 277, April 16, 1997, pp.
1224–28.

43. The 1,013 faculty and the 121 technology managers were from
the disciplines of biology, chemistry, computer science, and electrical
engineering and physics. Rahm, "University Linkages for Industrial
Innovation."

44. Cohen, Florida, and Goe, "University-Industry Research Centers in the United States."

45. Note that respondents may have interpreted the phrase, "information to be deleted from research papers," broadly to include proprietary information originating from the firms themselves, as distinct from
academic research findings. If this were the case, the propriety of restricting the disclosure of such information is apparent.

46. As background to these findings concerning disclosure restrictions, the results of the 1994 Carnegie Mellon Survey of Industrial R&D
suggest that between 1983 and 1994 firms came to rely much more
heavily on secrecy to protect their profits from innovation. Wesley M.
Cohen, Richard R. Nelson, and John Walsh, "Appropriability Conditions and Why Firms Patent and Why They Do Not in the American
Manufacturing Sector," Carnegie Mellon University, 1997.

47. Wesley M. Cohen, Richard Florida, and Lucien Randazzese, *For
Knowledge and Profit: University-Industry R&D Centers in the United States*
(forthcoming). It is important to reinforce exactly what the results from
tables 7–5 and 7–6 do and do not reveal. Table 7–5 refers only to whether
UIRCs permit publication restrictions, not whether such restrictions

were implemented. Table 7–6 refers to whether UIRCs ever imposed specific communication restrictions, not whether such restrictions were routinely or commonly imposed.

48. National Science Board, *Science and Engineering Indicators.*

49. Cohen, Florida, and Goe, "University-Industry Research Centers in the United States."

50. Cohen, Florida and Goe, "University-Industry Research Centers in the United States"; and Cohen, Florida, and Randazzese, "University-Industry Research Centers in Biotechnology."

51. Adams, "Fundamental Stocks of Knowledge and Productivity Growth."

52. Blumenthal and others, "Relationships between Academic Institutions and Industry"; and Cohen, Florida, and Goe, "University-Industry Research Centers in the United States."

Chapter 8

The Future of
Research Universities

Roger G. Noll

The preceding chapters do not support optimistic conclusions about the future of the American research university. How bleak is the forecast?

Federal support for university research certainly is not likely to grow as rapidly in the coming years as it has during most of the postwar era; most likely it will shrink slightly in inflation-adjusted dollars. Federal officials are likely to respond to stagnant or declining appropriations for research by continuing to force universities to share more of the costs on federal grants and by imposing ever more binding restrictions on indirect cost rates. University medical centers will inevitably suffer substantial budget pressures as both public and private purchasers of health care services attempt to contain the costs of health care. Many universities are likely to experience serious financial pressures affecting their entire budgets, not just their medical schools.

State governments began cutting their support for universities around 1990, and there is no reason to believe this trend will be reversed. Businesses have become an increasingly important source of support for universities. At the same time, the profit orientation of business not only limits the size and scope of this support, but also threatens the open structure of the university environment, thereby making business dollars less valuable than support from sources that have more altruistic purposes.

The one bright spot during the past few years has been student enrollment. Driven by the rising earnings premium that is attributable to higher education, university enrollments have increased despite rising tuition and the declining number of college-age adults. Similarly, the international dominance of U.S. universities and attractive job prospects for well-educated workers, especially in research-intensive industries, have encouraged a large number of foreign students to enroll in U.S. universities, especially in graduate science and engineering programs. Most of these students have remained in the United States, and they account for a large and growing share of employment in highly technical occupations.

If these trends do not change dramatically, research universities will be very different in the not-so-distant future. Facing declining overall budgets, universities cannot sustain the quality of their research. Moreover, because research and education appear to be complementary, rather than substitutes, declining support for research will have a deleterious effect on education, especially in technical disciplines, where opportunities for on-the-job training in a university research lab are likely to shrink.

The reductions in both research and technical education are likely to have a detrimental effect on economic growth, especially in high-technology industries. These consequences will be partially offset by changes in the orientation of universities to place more emphasis on teaching. If research universities shrink, the earnings premium attributable to higher education can be expected to grow. Complementing this source of increased demand will be the recently enacted tuition tax credit, which will increase students' ability to pay for college. As a result, universities can partially offset the reductions in other sources of revenues by raising tuition and using these funds to compete for students by investing in educational activities. The net effect of all of these changes is likely to be fewer well-educated students and higher tuition than would have been the case had support for research not declined; however, the educational activities of research universities probably will not deteriorate as much as their research output.

Another likely change is greater disparity in the quality of research universities. Institutions with a large endowment, no medical school, and many successful alumni will experience a much smaller percentage reduction in their budgets than institutions that have depended more heavily on federal grants, state appropriations, and profits from medical care. The most prestigious institutions should remain exceptionally strong and continue to be world leaders. Likewise, the best public institutions can continue to offset reductions in other sources of revenue by raising tuition and being more aggressive in private fund-raising.

Whereas a precise estimate is not feasible, most of the top twenty to thirty institutions are likely to remain strong. Beyond this group, opportunities for offsetting the decline in revenues resulting from reductions in government support and in the sale of medical care services are far more limited. Most likely, these institutions will make the most aggressive attempts to preserve their quality by reorienting themselves to support proprietary research for industry. This path is precarious because of the uncertainty surrounding the potential scope of business support.

Only two policy recommendations implied by this book do not require greater public expenditures. One is to streamline the accounting procedures for paying the indirect costs of federally sponsored research. This change could benefit universities by reducing their expenditures on complying with federal accounting rules, thereby increasing the amount of research and education that is produced from a dollar of federal expenditures. The other is to relax the tough standards for visas for both foreign students and highly educated foreigners who seek to remain in the United States, especially in highly technical fields that are in great demand in high-technology industries. Whereas neither policy would likely offset all the other trends, both could produce significant benefits for university budgets as well as increase education and research outputs.

As recounted in chapter one, many previous prophecies of doom for American universities have proven to be false. Unfavorable events that were interpreted as trends turned out to be only a short-term dip in the long-term growth trend for all colleges and universities. The same could be true of the 1990s. If so, where could the analysis in this book be mistaken?

The most likely source of error is in projecting recent trends in government expenditures far into the future. Federal support for research has declined primarily because of the end of the cold war and the resulting decline in defense expenditures. To date no issue has arisen that can substitute for national security as the galvanizing basis of support for science and engineering research at universities. A plausible candidate is personnel shortages and escalating salaries in high-technology industries as the supply of well-educated scientists and engineers falls. If industry advocates increased support for universities, the trends in federal research could be reversed. Similarly, industry could help to reverse the trend in declining state appropriations, although in this case research universities must compete for funds with elementary and secondary education, community colleges, and state teaching universities, all of which are more important sources of workers than research universities.

The organization and management of research universities have escaped analysis. Although there is no concrete evidence on the point, during the postwar era of rapid growth in all sources of revenues, universities may have accumulated organizational slack. If so, significant cuts could be made without reducing the quality of education or research by eliminating nonperforming programs and unnecessary administrative units. In reality, many universities have undertaken significant reorganizations and budget cuts in recent years, which is both good news and bad news. The good news is that other universities may be able to do the same; the bad news is that universities that have already gone through reorganization may have little left to cut.

The least likely source of error is the bleak forecast for university medical schools. The revolution in the way the nation pays for medical care is extremely unlikely to be reversed, meaning that revenues from patients in university hospitals and clinics will never again pay for as much education and research in medical schools as they did in the 1980s. The most secure forecast is that major financial problems are in store for universities that have depended on revenues from medical services to finance other parts of their operation.

The future of the research university, then, is one of challenge but not desperation. The very best institutions probably will weather the storm, perhaps shrinking slightly and undergoing a small reduction in quality, but their relative strength compared with other institutions of higher education could even make them better eventually, as the best students and faculty become more concentrated in the top institutions. The most threatened institutions are the below-average research universities that have a large medical school, a small endowment, and a small base of wealthy alumni. Some of these institutions may well abandon the attempt to be research universities.

Contributors

Gary Burtless, Brookings Institution

Linda R. Cohen, Department of Economics, University of California, Irvine

Wesley Cohen, Department of Social and Decision Sciences, Carnegie Mellon University

Richard Florida, Heinz School of Policy and Management, Carnegie Mellon University

Roger G. Noll, Department of Economics, Stanford University

Lucien Randazzese, Dean and Company

William P. Rogerson, Department of Economics, Northwestern University

Albert H. Teich, American Association for the Advancement of Science

John Walsh, Department of Sociology, University of Illinois at Chicago

Index